FAITH
H&EVERYTHING IN BETWEENPE
LOVE

FAITH
HOPE
& EVERYTHING IN BETWEEN
LOVE

MICK BROOKS

CWR

Concept development, editing, design and production by CWR
Printed in Finland by Bookwell
ISBN: 978-1-85345-598-8

CONTENTS

FOREWORD

What you hold in your hands is one of the most practical and well-written books for living the Christian life to come along in years. It comes from the pen of Mick Brooks, who leads the ministry at CWR, and it is a piece of work that would have made Selwyn proud and justified in his choice of a man who would continue his legacy. This book is also a reminder that CWR and the foundations laid by Selwyn Hughes are in good hands – alive and well.

Mick Brooks, Chief Executive and Ministry Director of CWR, has blessed the Church of God throughout the world by his clear and simple distillation of practical, biblical truths for both new Christians and those more established in their faith, even perhaps relating also to a person who has no knowledge of God whatever. There is a freshness in these pages that will delight the reader from start to finish. Filled with humour based upon his personal experiences, borrowing from the best of modern writers and mirroring the mind of Selwyn Hughes, Mick has provided new and mature Christians from every denominational and theological perspective with a piece of work that will bless thousands of lives.

What we have in this volume, then, is timely teaching for church leaders and all Christians who wish to reach those who are in the utterly secular world and have no understanding of the Christian faith. This book contains some rather sobering reminders to some of us who are so theological that we forget that it is not our orthodoxy or the doctrine of atonement, for example, that people out there are interested in but whether we *care*. Mick Brooks shows the difference faith, hope and love can make, whether it be a young boy praying for his playground enemy (and they become friends!) or of one thoughtful lady patting a child on the head with love – this leading her mother to want to come to church.

I possibly appreciated most of all Mick's emphasis on prayer and Bible reading – a discipline that has almost perished from the earth – the importance of having a prayer list and developing an intimacy with the Holy Spirit. This is what makes the Christian life a thrilling journey and not just our final destination. I pray that this book will be a blessing to you as you accept that the journey is what you are on already and not something you intend to start later! I urge you to accept the privilege of this journey and develop a love for stillness and fellowship with God – a blessed fringe benefit of knowing your final destination.

R.T. Kendall,
Minister, Westminster Chapel (1977–2002)
Hendersonville, Tennessee
June 2011

INTRODUCTION

'Life is a journey, not a destination.'

Ralph Waldo Emerson

'Life is not a problem to be solved but a mystery to be lived.'

Unknown

We all know that life can be unpredictable. Sometimes we love being alive, and feel joyful and exhilarated. At other times our existence can appear mundane, difficult or even painful. Whoever we are and however we feel about our lives right now, it is a safe bet to say that all of us are looking for lives of significance and value. None of us wants to live pointlessly. We want our time on earth to count for something. Looking for meaning, many of us would like our relationships and our work to 'make a difference' to those around us and, ultimately, to tie in with the purposes of God.

But in order to live life to the full, we need to ask some fundamental questions about where we are headed and why. For centuries philosophers, theologians, writers, preachers and taxi drivers have sought answers to the really BIG questions that sometimes keep us awake at night, such as, 'Who am I? Why am I alive? Is there a God?' (and 'Why do people persist in making daytime television?') Throughout this book I'll be suggesting we consider some similarly challenging questions that I hope will guide us into a deeper knowledge of God's truth.

I have very clear childhood memories of being given the book *The Pilgrim's Progress* by a Sunday school teacher. The story totally gripped me, which was amazing for a boy who at the time only read comic books. I found its vivid picture language played out in my imagination and was helpful for giving insights into people and life in general. But the book's biggest revelation to me was that life is about embarking on a gripping, adventurous journey, not just arriving at a final destination.

The journey of life has many twists and turns, many unfathomable, unforgettable and sometimes unpalatable moments. All of these are experiences that I passionately believe are vital to our growth as individuals, and as the collective people of God. The good news is that God does not leave us to face these things alone. He does not send us on ahead of Him or rush off and ask us to play catch up. I agree with Mother Teresa when she declared, 'God is on the journey, too.'

In the following pages I will seek to unpack some of the lessons I have learnt, and am still learning, about this amazing life we are privileged to lead. There is a divine pattern in place and a divine pacesetter walking with us. I believe there are a number of keys to living our Christian lives *well*. How we handle these will determine how well we journey. Come with me as I explore matters of faith, doubt, hope and loss. I am very aware that I don't have all the answers, because I am on my journey too. But, as Winston Churchill wrote:

> Every day you may make progress. Every step may be fruitful. Yet there will stretch out before you an ever-lengthening, ever-ascending, ever-improving path. You know you will never get to the end of the journey. But this, so far from discouraging, only adds to the joy and glory of the climb.

I hope you enjoy walking through these pages with me. May the God of all our pilgrimages help us to progress in the way He desires.

life's JOURNEY

'*The journey is the reward.*'

CHINESE PROVERB

01

THE JOURNEY TOWARDS HOLINESS

There was once a man called Jim who, in his late seventies, was asked to share his testimony. Well known as a man of faith and a seasoned prayer warrior, Jim stood at the microphone at the front of the church. His first sentence surprised his hearers: 'I became a Christian when I was a very young boy. The Lord knew He had so much work to do in me, He decided to start early.' Jim was deadly serious as he humbly declared how God had transformed him, little by little, for the last sixty-five years of his life. Many of those listening were moved by the story of his personal journey. They changed their minds about Jim, looking at him differently. Rather than seeing a man who had always been godly, they realised, for the first time, that he had spent a lifetime travelling towards holiness. The beautiful sculpture in front of them was the result of years of heavenly chiselling.

THE JOURNEY TOWARDS MATURITY

For many years I was sure that each person's spiritual journey towards God was unique. I believed it was a personal marathon on an uncharted map, and that each person of faith was on a different walk of a different nature. Now, however, after knowing and walking alongside (or rather trying to keep in step with) Jesus for a good many years, my opinion has changed. It's amazing what difference the presence of a rear-view mirror makes – not just to the view of things behind us, but to the speed with which we journey along the road in front.

Sadly, none of us are born mature. We need to learn, grow and develop in order to reach our potential and be made more like Christ. We don't all travel along the road of our discipleship at the same rate. Some lessons we will take longer than our peers to learn. Occasionally, we will find something easy whilst another person struggles to grasp it. We are all unique. But although our growth rate is different, there are certain things we all face and deal with as we mature in our Christian walk. Certain principles remain constant, even if they are parcelled in personal vocabulary, experiences and wisdom.

So what does movement towards God look like? First of all, most of our growth in Christ is not glamorous. Many days of our Christian lives are not, in themselves, amazing, miraculous, or appear to be anything extraordinary. We are not going to feed the five thousand with every packed lunch we are given, or experience the manifest presence of God in every prayer meeting. Perhaps you have read some Christian books that describe another believer's life in almost superhuman terms? Chapter One is where they have breakfast with some angels before raising the dead by coffee-time! We can put down such books thinking, 'I'll never be like that!' and maybe conclude that God will never be able to use us to do anything significant.

That feeling is so common, but it is not actually true. God has a purpose for each one of us that only we can fulfil. His journey for me is not His journey for you. I need my own. You need yours. The story is told in 1 Samuel 17 of how David went before King Saul, offering to fight Israel's oppressor, Goliath. Saul accepted David's offer, then promptly dressed him in his armour (v.38). The trouble was, the armour wasn't designed for David. It didn't fit properly and was burdensome and heavy. The armour hampered David's movement, and he couldn't get going until he took it off. Similarly, God knows that for each situation we face in life, there are certain things that we need. But it is *His* job to provide them.

Much of what we go through in life feels like the 'ups and downs' of normal living. We have mortgages to pay, jobs to do, washing machines that break down, parents who become ill, ministries that appear to wane. It's all part of life. We can sometimes fall into the trap of saying, 'Why has this happened to me?' or 'How did this occur?' forgetting to consider the plans and purposes of God. Perhaps we have put off certain things – 'After Christmas, I will sort out my weight', or 'When the children are grown up, I will deal with my marriage problems'. We can spend so much time wishing life away, or hoping to arrive somewhere different, that we don't embrace or learn from the journey or truly realise where we *are*. It really helps to remember that the Christian life is as much about *travelling* as it is about arriving. Father Alfred D'Souza once put it like this:

> For a long time it had seemed to me that life was about to begin – real life. But there was always some obstacle in the way, something to be gotten through first, some unfinished business, time still to be served, a debt to be paid. Then life would begin. At last it dawned on me that these obstacles *were* my life.

There is, I believe, a divine pattern at work which, whilst allowing the widest variety for each person and their own individuality, seeks to bring us towards union with God through spiritual encounters and experiences which are common to us all. Mike Riddell says:

> It's a mistake to think that destination is the most important part. The most insufferable people are those who think they have arrived, and trade their shoes for a comfortable bed … we were made with hunger for the road in our gut. Best to face it.

The phrase 'spiritual formation' is becoming increasingly popular in Christian culture and communities. Put simply, it refers to the way God goes about producing the image of Christ within us. His goal is not just that I journey towards Him, but that while on the way I begin to both look like and act like Him, reflecting His character and nature. He will use every person, situation and circumstance in my life to make that happen.

THE JOURNEY OF EMPOWERMENT

Currently, I have the privilege of leading CWR, the ministry begun by Selwyn Hughes in the 1960s. When I first joined, I began on a six-month contract. I had no idea that twenty years later I would still be here and that my own life and calling would be still focused on this ministry. But God clearly had His plans and ideas. He faithfully started a 'great work' in Selwyn and is continuing it today in CWR in many diverse ways. From a new counselling degree with university accreditation to a range of devotionals for young people, CWR is constantly changing and adapting to the needs of those it serves, as it follows the leading of God. This same God who has proved Himself faithful to me – both in the ministry I work with, and in my own personal journey with Him – has proved and will prove Himself faithful to you. He is the Lord of the journey – the great I AM.

Being a Christian is a long walk, not a short race. We need God's strength to continue on it and to finish it strong. As a young Christian, Selwyn was told that having been *made new* by the Spirit he now needed the *empowering* of the Spirit. Following advice from his elders, he sought God. The encounter he experienced with the Holy Spirit did indeed transform him. He then asked the elders what to do next. 'That's it!' they said, as if there were nothing else he had to do in the Christian life – as if he'd arrived spiritually! But life's experience showed him there was still much to do and to learn. And for each of us, even though we are indwelt by the Spirit of God and empowered by Him, we still have many areas in which to grow, learn and mature. As Christians, disciples of Jesus, we have been called to 'work out' and 'walk out' those great works of our Father. Like Jesus, we need to continually learn to see what our Father is seeing and do what our Father is doing.

> Jesus gave them this answer: 'I tell you the truth, the Son can do nothing by himself; he can do only what he sees his Father doing, because whatever the Father does the Son also does.'
>
> **John 5:19**

I often stand amazed and humbled at God's consistent willingness to continue to use me. I sometimes find myself questioning, 'How on earth did I get here, God? Why did this opportunity come my way?' I have learnt that my task is to follow where He leads me as faithfully as I can.

THE JOURNEY OF FOLLOWING

In Genesis 12:1 we read about God's call to Abram:

> The LORD had said to Abram, 'Leave your country, your people and your father's household and go to the land I will show you.'

Note that God did not give Abraham a postcode or a final destination. He simply told him to 'Go!' and then assured him, 'I will show you the way, step by step.' Our calling is to follow God's leading in this same way. We sometimes expect God to be a divine sat nav or GPS showing us the shortest or fastest route to the final destination. Like Christian in *The Pilgrim's Progress*, we find that life is often an adventure. We don't always know where God is going to lead us at any particular time. Sometimes the road is far from comfortable, straight and certain, but we are never on it alone.

God is committed to working in your life. More than this, God is committed to you! Even though we sometimes don't realise it, don't feel like it's true and even, at times, don't want it, God is committed to finishing what He has started. He takes imperfect people and works constantly to transform us, using everything we go through as the tools of His trade.

THE JOURNEY OF THE PILGRIM

The early believers were not called Christians or even disciples. Known as 'The people of the Way' because it was as if they were on a constant pilgrimage, these first converts lived lives that embraced change and movement. I find that an exciting, but sometimes daunting prospect. However, their very name is in line with the itinerant nature of Jesus who described Himself as having 'nowhere to lay his head' (Luke 9:58). Jesus was constantly on the move, going from town to town, house to house and person to person.

Much of the Bible tells stories of people making important journeys. Abraham and Sarah left their home in Ur and set out on a journey. Moses led the Jews out of Egypt to the promised land. Jesus sent His disciples out into the towns to share their faith. Saul was transformed into Paul as he journeyed on the road to Damascus. Two disciples met Jesus as they journeyed on the road to Emmaus.

St Richard's prayer on his deathbed was reported to be this:

Thanks be to you, my Lord, Jesus Christ, for all the benefits that you have given me; for all the pains and insults you have borne for me. O, most merciful redeemer, friend and brother, may I know you more clearly; love you more dearly; and follow you more nearly.[1]

This sense of 'following more nearly' and of walking closely with God is what our faith journey is all about. Being in close proximity to a holy God equips us for a life of holiness too. But we are never alone in our attempts. God is our constant companion, our very 'near' friend.

To journey as a pilgrim is to experience many opposites in tandem: healing and hurt, faith and doubt, grace and judgment, wholeness and brokenness. Pilgrims do not escape the trials and tribulations of life, but each of us who embraces the journey knows that to walk the pilgrim's way is to live fully and to be fully alive.

THE JOURNEY TOWARDS STILLNESS

The society in which we live doesn't have too much of an understanding of the concept of journeying. We live in a consumerist society where we buy something, use it and then throw it away. We are in too much of a hurry. We want to get everything done *now*. Have you ever stood in front of a microwave and thought, 'Come on, hurry up!'? It's sad, isn't it? I sometimes find myself thinking, 'I wish God would hurry up and do this!' It's easy to become a 'microwave' or 'boil in the bag' Christian. When it comes to spiritual maturity, spiritual discipleship and spiritual formation, we want it done yesterday! We want to know the Bible, but can't be bothered to actually read it. We want God to answer our prayers, but we don't make time to pray consistently. We want to gain wisdom and understanding, but we don't read books or talk with those who have gained it. No wonder we end up with some half-baked theology and wonder where God is at times. Instead we need to take a slower, simmering approach to transformation.

The Christian life is not just a spiritual journey, it includes a physical journey too, a notion more popular historically than today, often taking the form of pilgrimages. In the sixth century, Irish Celtic monks, in imitation of Abraham, developed the discipline of *peregrinatio* from the Latin meaning 'going forth into strange countries'. This understanding of pilgrimage was different to normal medieval pilgrimage, namely, a visit to a sacred site or shrine. The purpose of all medieval pilgrimage had been simply to 'arrive' somewhere else. But these monks challenged that understanding. The purpose of these Irish pilgrimages was not to visit some holy shrine or to arrive at a certain destination, but to seek out the very presence of God in solitude, mystery, exile and freedom. 'So crucial was this idea of total abandonment to God,' writes Rev Doctor John Montgomery, 'that these Irish pilgrims often set out on their journey not knowing their destination, relying solely on the Spirit to guide them to the place God would have them go.'[2]

We are all *peregrini pro Christo*, pilgrims for Christ, and our journeys take differing forms. Maybe right now God is whispering, trying to get your attention, or talking loud and clear to you about your future. Perhaps He is asking you to make a step of faith to another place for Him. I see the Christian life like this. Many times in my own life, I have looked at where I am on my journey with God, and realised that I did not choose that place on my 'itinerary' to visit. Where I have arrived is not a final destination, but is still a place of worth and meaning, a place where God intended me to be.

Realising where we are is part of our maturing. It is about a deeper relationship and connection to God, to our inner self, and to others. Our pilgrim's path may take us into some dark valleys or up high mountains. We may find ourselves in the midst of confusion, illness, grief or pain, or find we have so much joy we cannot contain it. Perhaps we are led to work through a strained relationship rather than walk away from it, or maybe we volunteer at a homeless shelter and meet someone who changes our lives. God has a habit of surprising us and working through all things.

Sometimes we may have to take ourselves away from ordinary routines and practices in order to seek a closer 'first love' connection with God and His Word and 'arrive at where we started'. This can be a demanding task. For many of us, stopping being so active and busy, and allowing ourselves time to 'be' can bring an odd sense of disconnection. And yet, when we allow stillness into our lives, radical things can happen. Our growth often takes place in secret, quiet places.

THE JOURNEY OF DISCIPLESHIP

Did you ever play the game 'Follow my Leader' at school? The whole point of it is not to watch what other people are doing, but to keep your eyes on the person in front. Jesus doesn't always tell us where to go or where He is going. When we are born again we do not receive a full-scale business plan for each moment of the rest of our lives. He just says 'Follow Me!' and places a calling on our lives. We need to overcome the temptation to follow other people, and instead keep our eyes fixed on Him.

I often feel intimidated when I look at the characters in Scripture. They just seem to be incredible. They take whole cities for God armed only with trumpets and jam jars. Their lives are full of burning bushes and pillars of cloud. They are doing miracles left, right and through the centre of 'Red' seas. So, I found the following letter helpful:

To: Jesus, son of Joseph
Woodcrafter,
Carpenter shop,
Nazareth.

From Jordan Management Consultants

Dear Sir,

Thank you for submitting resumés of the twelve men you have picked for management positions in your new organisation. All of them have now taken our battery of tests. We not only ran the results through our computer, but also arranged personal interviews for each of them with our psychologist and vocational aptitude consultant. It is our opinion that most of your nominees are lacking in the background, education and vocational aptitude for the type of enterprise you are undertaking. They do not have the team concept. We would recommend that you continue your search for persons of experience in managerial ability and proven capability.

Simon Peter is unstable and given to fits of temper.

Andrew has absolutely no qualities of leadership.

The two brothers, James and John, the sons of Zebedee, place personal interest above company loyalty.

Thomas demonstrates a questioning attitude that would tend to undermine morale.

We feel it is our duty to tell you that Matthew has been blacklisted by the Greater Jerusalem Better Business Bureau.

James, the son of Alpheus, and Thaddeus definitely have radical leanings, and are frequently highly emotional.

Simon the Zealot, having pronounced extremist
leanings, would blow apart the harmony of the team.
One of the candidates however, shows great potential.
He is a man of great ability and resourcefulness, meets
people well, has a keen business mind, and has contacts
in high places. He is highly motivated, ambitious and
responsible. We recommend Judas Iscariot as your
controller and right hand man. All of the other profiles
are self-explanatory.
We wish you every success in your new venture.
Sincerely yours
Jordan Management Consultants[3]

I don't know about you, but I'm grateful Jesus didn't require me to complete an aptitude test to qualify as one of His followers. Fortunately, He knows our end from our beginning. There is a saying, 'Every saint has a past and every sinner has a future'. God knows what we can be. He has put His hope in us and we can trust Him.

THE JOURNEY TOWARDS DESTINY

We need to remind ourselves that the journey of faith is like the one made by the prodigal son. We leave behind the 'pig pen' of self-reliance, self-rule and selfishness, and travel towards the outstretched arms of the Father.

The journey that each of us is on with God is all about change. Not simply a change of scene or a change of clothes (as a physical journey), but often a change of heart, attitudes, dreams and mind. Are you ready for God to challenge and stir you, and to lead you into this next stage of your personal journey?

With the Israelites, God had much more in mind than just deliverance from slavery; He had in mind deliverance from themselves and a journey towards real closeness with Him. He was not just leading them into a new land but into a new relationship, revealing Himself as the God who kept His promises along the way.

Jesus, too, spoke to His disciples with this intent:

> And He said to them, 'Come after Me [as disciples – letting Me be your Guide], follow Me, and I will make you fishers of men!'
>
> **Matt. 4:19, Amplified**

Jesus is not talking here simply about a *destination*, but a destiny. If we follow Him, He will *make* us what we were intended to be – a royal priesthood and a chosen people (1 Pet. 2:9). The very essence of following Jesus is this journey of transformation – a journey of becoming some-*one* and not just doing some-*thing*.

THE JOURNEY OF REMEMBERING

Faith isn't necessarily the absence of doubt. Doubt can be a very positive thing. The opposite of faith is sometimes certainty. Think about it: if you know something beyond a shadow of doubt, you are not exercising faith any more!

For me, a large part of faith has to do with remembering the goodness of God. The trouble is, I can so often forget how amazing God is and go wandering off in my own direction. Then, like Christian in *The Pilgrim's Progress*, I meet those who try to distract me from my journey, and I fall into difficulty. One of the reasons that we are so fearful in the presence of new danger and new situations is simply because we've forgotten how good God was to us in the past.

The human heart is crippled by forgetfulness. All through the Old Testament you hear God telling the children of Israel not to forget, to make monuments as a physical reminder of His presence and power. Deuteronomy 4:9 says:

> 'Only be careful, and watch yourselves closely so that you do not forget the things your eyes have seen or let them slip from your heart as long as you live. Teach them to your children and to their children after them.'

How often do you forget what God has done for you? It is so easy to do. God has doubtless spoken to you numerous times in your life, but how many of these occasions can you remember? Over the years I've had several encounters with God – enough, at one level, to provide me with a lifetime of conviction. So why don't I live more faithfully? It is simply because I forget.

The ultimate story of forgetting – that of the golden calf in Exodus 32 – is quite phenomenal. If you think about the background of what happened before this incident, where the Israelites had seen so many astonishing things, it is surprising that they forgot *so* quickly.

They had seen the Red Sea open miraculously, they had drunk water from a rock, they had eaten food that fell from the sky. You would think that would have been convincing enough, wouldn't you? Every day God had faithfully supplied them with all their needs (just as He does yours and mine). Moses goes up Mount Sinai and there's so much thunder going on that the people shake in their sandals (Exod. 19:16)! But he is only gone for ten days and what do they do? They build a golden calf. They decide that they need something to worship, so they melt down all their gold, fashion an idol and bow down to it. They've forgotten all those things that God has seen them through. It's astonishing.

But in the same situation, would you and I be any different? I doubt it! Our memories are very short and we easily forget what we should remember. It was Martin Lloyd Jones who commented that we would even forget the Lord's death were it not for the reminder provided by the Communion. Jesus asked us to do that for a reason! From Genesis to Revelation the Bible is full of calls to remember.

What is your golden calf? What do you hang on to in place of God when He appears to be out of sight? Have you forgotten the goodness of God because the clouds of your circumstances are preventing you from seeing Him clearly?

There were three ladies talking about getting older. One of them said, 'Sometimes I find myself with a jar of mayonnaise in my hand, and I'm standing by the fridge door and it's like, was I putting it away or was I making a sandwich?' Her friend said, 'Yes! Sometimes I find myself on the landing of the stairs and I can't remember whether I was coming up or going down.' The third friend replied, 'Well, I don't have any of those kinds of problems.' As she spoke she rapped her knuckles emphatically on the table. The noise she made surprised her. 'Hang on,' she cried, getting up. 'There must be somebody at the door!' We so quickly forget.

Selwyn Hughes once went to pray with a lady in his church whose husband was really ill. The elders joined him in praying for the man, and anointed him with oil. Then they turned and said to his wife, 'We've done all that we can do. We now have to simply trust God.' 'Oh dear!' she responded, 'Has it come to that?'

Many of us only turn to God as a last resort because we've forgotten His goodness in our lives. But the Bible shows us time and time again that He never forgets us even when we forget or turn from Him.

I thank God for the path He has taken me on. I might change one or two things, make a few tweaks here and there, but I am so grateful to God for His persistent goodness to me. Do you intentionally and actively try to remember the goodness of God? Do you have faith to trust in Him even if things in your life are far from how you'd like them to be? May I recommend that you start writing things down to jog your memory? You'll be amazed at all God has done.

THE JOURNEY OF SALVATION

Romans 8:29–30 in *The Message* says this:

> God knew what he was doing from the very beginning. He decided from the outset to shape the lives of those who love him along the same lines as the life of his Son. The Son stands first in the line of humanity he restored. We see the original and intended shape of our lives there in him. After God made that decision of what his children should be like, he followed it up by calling people by name. After he called them by name, he set them on a solid basis with himself. And then, after getting them established, he stayed with them to the end, gloriously completing what he had begun.

Many have tended to view salvation in purely legal or judicial terms. But this is far from the whole story. Salvation is not just about contractual law. God's salvation is deeply relational and 'restorational' because He is a deeply relational, restoring God. We can say we are saved and it sounds as if the all the work has been done (and in a sense that is true). But can we say, 'I'm saved, that's it – there's nothing more to do'?

I have always liked the old story of a group of young Christians who came from a church where they regarded clerical attire and the wearing of robes as inappropriate and the trappings of liberalism. They were giving out gospel tracts in the town when they saw a minister wearing a clerical collar coming towards them. One of them whispered to another, 'Go and ask him if he is saved!' So the vicar was asked the question. With a twinkle in his eye he responded, 'Yes and no. If you mean am I saved from the *penalty* of sin then the answer is yes. If you mean am I saved from the *power* of sin then the answer is yes *and* no. The power of sin has been largely broken in my life, but there is still some way to go. If you mean am I saved from the *presence* of sin the answer is most definitely no. That is something I wait for with eager anticipation. Now, does that answer your question?' The young man who had asked the question swallowed hard, excused himself and went back to his friends like a dog with his tail between his legs, feeling somewhat embarrassed.

There has been a tendency, albeit unconsciously, amongst some Christians to see the Christian life in terms of a one-off commitment and a set of obligations with an emphasis on prayer, Bible reading, church involvement and so on, rather than a transformational journey that will lead to a deeper understanding of the living God. Dallas Willard commented on the attitude of many believers saying, 'The current gospel becomes a "gospel of sin management".'[4]

In other words, the Christian life can become primarily focused on how we get on top of the problem of sin that keeps occurring in our lives. There is no doubt that this is an important issue, but there is so much more to the Christian life than that! Jesus did not go to the cross just to deal with your sin and mine. Nor are we simply waiting to go to heaven and filling the time as best we can! Jesus went to the cross so that we could *know* Him, the Father and the Spirit in true *koinonia* (fellowship), not just now but forever. This is the journey we are all on – the journey of faith, hope, love and everything in between.

We sometimes seem to have so focused on exuberant beginnings and victorious endings that we have forgotten about the slow unravelling of God's grace that takes place each day. As Paul puts it in 2 Corinthians 3:16–18:

... when God is personally present, a living Spirit, that
old, constricting legislation is recognized as obsolete.
We're free of it! All of us! Nothing between us and God,
our faces shining with the brightness of his face. And so we
are transfigured much like the Messiah, our lives gradually
becoming brighter and more beautiful as God enters our
lives and we become like him.

The Message

In other words, God is so excited about Jesus that He wants to make
everyone like Him. Not physically, of course, but in terms of character,
ethics and virtues. And it is the way that God goes about the task
of producing the image of His Son Jesus in us which is spiritual
formation. All the challenges that we face and the questions we ask
are part of that process.

MAKING THE MOST OF THE JOURNEY

The older I get the more I wonder where the time seems to go. There are
a worrying number of slogans I now relate to: 'You are only as old as
you feel! ... Life begins at forty/fifty! ... Those aren't wrinkles, they're
expression lines ...' You know the ones? All I can say is that I seem to
have developed a lot of expression as time has gone on! Someone once
lyrically expressed this sentiment:

I get up in the morning and I dust off my wits,
I go out and get the paper and read the obits.
If my name is missing I know I'm not dead.
So I eat a good breakfast and go back to bed.

Anonymous

The speaker and author Jeff Lucas announced a while ago at the annual Spring Harvest conference, 'I have calculated that I have spent many months of my life living in a Butlins chalet!' What a thought!

I have since discovered that we spend the equivalent of three years of our life in school (that's twenty-four hours a day), five years travelling, one year recovering from sickness and five years talking. We spend twenty-four years sleeping and fifteen years pursuing leisure activities. But get this: if we spent *every* Sunday in church without ever missing a service and we went to a midweek meeting, too, that only comes to five and a half months! Isn't that interesting? We need to make the most of the journey we are given and learn from every aspect of our days, months and years, not just our Sundays.

Another fascinating part of making the most of our Christian walk comes when we realise we are not alone. When we receive Jesus into our lives, we inherit a whole new family. We are meant to relate to them as we relate to Him. The difficulty is that sometimes those we are asked to call our 'brothers and sisters' are awkward, irritating or even downright obnoxious. However, I have learnt over time that the more I relate to others (even those difficult people I'd prefer were not in my church or neighbourhood), the more real God becomes to me. Human relationships have brought God closer to me and taught me more about His nature and His character.

THE JOURNEY WILL END

Philippians 1:1–6 says this:

> Paul and Timothy, servants of Christ Jesus, To all the saints in Christ Jesus at Philippi, together with the overseers and deacons: Grace and peace to you from God our Father and the Lord Jesus Christ. I thank my God every time I remember you.

In all my prayers for all of you, I always pray with joy because
of your partnership in the gospel from the first day until now,
being confident of this, that he who began a good work in you
will carry it on to completion until the day of Christ Jesus.

This is wonderfully reassuring – I hope this book will speak grace and
peace into your life as you explore and consider your own Christian
journey. I know that God says over you, just like the *Mastermind*
host and quizmaster always says as the buzzer goes, 'I've started, so
I'll finish ...' Or as *The Message* version of verse 6 says so clearly:

There has never been the slightest doubt in my mind that
the God who started this great work in you would keep at
it and bring it to a flourishing finish on the very day Christ
Jesus appears.

I love the idea that God, who after all started this great work, will
bring it to a 'flourishing finish', don't you? That is the destination
of each of our spiritual journeys. It is not just a hope, but a certain
promise at which we will eventually arrive.

1 Corinthians 13:12–13 says this:

We don't yet see things clearly. We're squinting in a fog,
peering through a mist. But it won't be long before the
weather clears and the sun shines bright! We'll see it all then,
see it all as clearly as God sees us, knowing him directly just
as he knows us! But for right now, until that completeness,
we have three things to do to lead us toward that
consummation: Trust steadily in God, hope unswervingly,
love extravagantly. And the best of the three is love.

The Message

What does maturity in God look like? I think it is remarkably like the last phrase of the passage I just quoted: 'To trust steadily, hope unswervingly and love extravagantly.' That just about sums it up. God is committed to finishing His work in you. Are you committed to letting Him start, or continue that process?

I pray new levels of trust, hope and love for you as you travel through these next few chapters with me.

life
THROUGH A LENS

'Are you really sure that a floor
can't also be a ceiling?'

M.C. ESCHER

02

'We've got a sort of brainwashing going on in our country,' Morrie sighed. 'Do you know how they brainwash people? They repeat something over and over. And that's what we do in this country. Owning things is good. More money is good. More property is good. More commercialism is good. More is good. More is good. We repeat it – and have it repeated to us – over and over until nobody bothers to even think otherwise. The average person is so fogged up by all of this, he has no perspective on what's really important anymore.

'Wherever I went in my life, I met people wanting to gobble up something new. Gobble up a new car. Gobble up a new piece of property. Gobble up the latest toy. And then they wanted to tell you about it. "Guess what I got? Guess what I got?"'[1]

THE BIG PICTURE

If I were to ask you what your world-view is, I wonder how you would answer. A person's view of the world colours how they perceive and comprehend everything around them. An individual's world-view is their 'big picture' – their way of understanding reality. Whether we realise it or not, our world-view is the benchmark we use for making all our daily decisions, for setting our goals and managing our time and relationships. It is therefore also extremely important to the way in which we view our Christian journey.

Let's take a simple example. Say I put a banana in front of you. Depending on who you are and what you do, that banana could mean different things. A scientist could classify it, an artist could draw it, a grocer could sell it and a child could eat it. But it is still a banana! How we look at any situation in front of us is influenced by how we look at the world at large. What we see depends on where we stand.

THE BIG LONGING

Most people, if they allow themselves to feel it, experience the sensation of not being quite at home in this world. There is a sense of dissatisfaction with things the way they are. I believe this is because something very important awaits us elsewhere. The writer Aldous Huxley said, 'Sooner or later one asks even of Beethoven, even of Shakespeare ... "Is this all?"' This has been described by C.S. Lewis as the 'inconsolable secret ... news from a country we have never visited.'[2]

It is not only Christians who experience these feelings. Augustine, the Christian philosopher and writer, spoke about this perception long before his conversion. C.S. Lewis struggled hard and fought against the idea that the source of his 'inconsolable longing' and the God of traditional religion might be one and the same. Of his search for God, Lewis said that they might as well talk about the mouse's search for the cat.[3] He later said that he was not made for here.[4]

How does the mass of humanity go about dealing with the underlying feeling of dissatisfaction and restlessness? One way is that we simply pretend that this mysterious unrecognised longing does not exist. It is strange that the soul's sense of homelessness is not studied more fully. I wonder why? Perhaps it is because it does not fit into the usual categories of thought. It cannot be successfully labelled, sorted, explained or matched, so men and women make a detour around it and pretend it is not there. Perhaps it is one of the greatest of all the enemy's assignments: to try to make us not even ask the question. But this detour or refusal is simply a denial.

THE BIG QUESTIONS

Most world-views, Christian or otherwise, will determine our outlook on life and will influence how we answer life's big questions, such as:

1. Where did we come from? (And why are we here?)
2. What is wrong with the world?
3. How can we 'fix' the world?

There are, of course, many religious world-views, influencing belief and behaviour. One of the most popular and prevalent current world-views is that of 'naturalism' which answers the questions above like this:

1. We are the product of random acts of nature with no real purpose.
2. We do not respect nature as we should.
3. We can ensure the world lasts longer through ecology and conservation, but we can never fix it.

A naturalistic world-view generates many related philosophies, some of which clash with one another. Books fill hundreds of library shelves on subjects such as moral relativism (the difference of moral or ethical standpoints in differing cultures), existentialism (that individuals are solely responsible for giving their lives meaning), pragmatism (those who claim that if something works, then it's right) and utopianism (those who intentionally try to create a perfect society).

THE BIG ANSWERS

A Christian world-view, on the other hand, would answer the same three questions from a biblical standpoint along the lines of:

1. We are God's creation, designed to govern the world and live in relationship and fellowship with Him and others (Gen. 1:27–28; 2:15).
2. We declared independence from God and brought creation under a curse (Gen. 3).
3. God redeemed the world through the sacrifice of His Son, Jesus Christ (Luke 19:10), broke the power of the curse (Gen. 3:15), and will one day restore creation to its former perfect state (Isa. 65:17–25).

A Christian world-view leads us to conclude that God can be known; that He has revealed Himself in His living Word, the Bible, and through continuing miracles; that He has overcome and answered every human need, and that He has given us the possibility of redemption and a chance to live in eternal communion with Him. And that's just for starters!

It is important to remember that a world-view is, by definition, comprehensive. It does not just affect how we speak or how we listen to someone else speaking. It influences just about every area of our life's journey, from the money we spend to the morals we live by; from our politics to the art on our walls; from where we go on holiday to what we watch on TV. Christianity is more than a set of ideas to pull out at Sunday school or think about for ten minutes a day in our 'quiet time' – far from it! The Bible never makes a distinction between a 'religious' and a 'secular' life: it refers simply to 'life'. In fact, the Christian life holds itself to be is the only real life there is. Jesus proclaimed Himself to be '*the* way and *the* truth and *the* life' (John 14:6, italics mine) and, in so doing, He actually became our world-view! (I could have just skipped writing this last piece and said, 'Jesus is the answer', because it's true.)

THE BIG LIE

I worked for a long time with people suffering from eating disorders. In the UK I heard many people saying, 'I'm not thin enough.' But in another country I worked in, I heard people in real distress saying the opposite – they wanted to be bigger! Without realising it, our view of ourselves is often dictated by those around us.

Let me ask you a couple of tough questions. Firstly, what do you think of yourself? And secondly, what is your purpose? As you try to answer those, examine what labels you wear and who helped create them for you. We look at both ourselves and the world around us through various lenses, such as education, experience, emotions, and everyone else's opinions. We can't help it. The trouble is, not everything we are told is in line with God's Word. As a result, we can end up believing all sorts of lies.

For example, have you ever said anything like this about yourself? 'I will never be any good at organising my time … I am not bright enough to go to university … I will never be able to trust anyone again … I've been too sinful for God to forgive me … I will never be healed … I don't think I'll ever marry … I'm stuck in this job forever … My son will never come home …'

The question is, are we dictated to by those perceptions of reality and carried along by what others have said over us, or can we begin to challenge and question what we have been told until we are aligned more fully to the revelations of Scripture?

I remember my first day at secondary school. Walking into the metalwork room, I was a small boy with a big imagination – there was nothing I couldn't create in this room, and it was incredible. But just as I walked in, minding my own business, the metalwork teacher swatted me across the backside with his metre-long ruler. I was taken completely by surprise by this and I won't repeat what I said at that particular time. The teacher said to me, 'I know your brother and I won't have any of it from you!' I made a pact with myself there and then, and I never attended another of his lessons. In fact, I didn't go to school much after that, if truth be told. Even today I can still remember the impact of those words.

God, however, does not look at us and see someone else. He looks at us and sees our journey, our ideas, our flaws, our strengths – and He loves us.

Think for a minute on a personal level of some of the voices you have listened to or gained your experience from. Maybe they were positive, maybe they were negative, maybe there is a voice that still rings in your head that says you are nothing, worth nothing and good for nothing. The biggest of all lies! A colleague of mine, Philip Greenslade, wrote:

> Let's ask this question. 'Who told you?' to the prodigal son in Jesus' story. Who told the prodigal son that he would best fulfil his potential as a human being by turning his back on the father who had given him birth and loved him? Who told him that freedom was best achieved by breaking free of the father's house and heart and going off to 'do your own thing'? Biblical scholars tell us that by asking for his share of the inheritance while his father was still alive, the son was in effect wishing his father dead!
>
> At what point did so many people in the modern world begin to believe that they would be better off if God was dead? ... And even when the prodigal comes to his senses, where did he get the false idea that the only reception his

father would give him would be the grudging acceptance as a hired hand rather than the full welcome of a returning son? Who told us lies about God's goodness and grace? Who led us into thinking that God was mean and ugly and vengeful? Where did we get those ideas from? Who convinced the older brother that serving dutifully was all the father wanted, that the father wasn't really interested in blessing him above the course of duty, that the father was really withholding the best from him and preferred keeping his nose to the religious grindstone? What made the son think the father so mean and ungenerous that it wouldn't be worth asking him for anything?[5]

God *is* goodness! He doesn't just show goodness. God *is* grace! He doesn't just demonstrate grace. He is who He says He is. So who has lied to you? It's the devil. He's not called the father of lies for nothing. We must tune our ears and our eyes to truth.

Paul summarises in Romans 1 our whole sinful predicament as believing a lie, believing a world-view that is alien to God's. A loving God probes our confusion and questions our ideals. He queries whether we are listening too much to the opinion-formers and reflectors in the media. I was recently watching a TV soap when one of the characters said something to the effect that women just want cheap wine and a compliment, to keep them happy. Six million people tune in several days a week watching and hearing those kind of statements. I read recently that by the age of eighteen most people will have watched somewhere in the region of 8–9,000 simulated acts of sex on the TV. Very rarely are those acts seen to take place within a loving, married relationship. Sex within marriage is often portrayed as dull and dismal. These media representations – or misrepresentations – can enormously affect our world-view.

It matters what we believe and why. It matters what we base our lives on. God is trustworthy. He speaks truth and He acts with truth. His Word is true and it leads to more truth for those who read and understand and live it.

I love the part in C.S Lewis's *The Lion, the Witch and the Wardrobe* when Lucy, talking of Aslan (the Jesus figure) asks if he is safe, and is told that no of course he isn't, but that he is good.

Have you been told God is mean? If God did not spare His only Son, but gave Him up for you, how will He not give us freely all things (see Rom. 8:32)? Has anyone ever told you that you are worthless? I tell you today you are valued by the cross of Jesus Christ! He has paid the price for you. Having done so much for you, God cannot love you any more and He cannot love you any less. He aims to redeem you and bring you into the fullness of your intended value. The cross speaks the truth to those who have ears to hear and hearts to believe.

THE BIG APPLE

We normally go to God and ask Him questions, don't we? But actually He asks some very interesting ones too. The second of the questions He asks of Adam in Genesis 3:11 is, 'Who told you?' What is really interesting is that Adam deflects this question and never answers it. He blames Eve instead. In fact, you could even argue that he blames God for the lie he believed. You've probably heard the saying, 'Adam blamed Eve, Eve blamed the serpent, and the serpent didn't have a leg to stand on!'

God still asks of us today, 'Who told you?' and this question incorporates a whole number of ideas and concepts. Who told you the world looked like this? Where do your ideas come from? What are they based on? Who has convinced you to think like this? Who has influenced your thinking over the years? What voices are you listening to? What is shaping the course of your life?

This question-asking incorporates what some commentators refer to as *epistemology*. It's talking about our world-view, our thinking and our values, our strategies and our choices. We all have a world-view which influences how we answer these questions:

1. When did I come to know what I know?
2. Why do I believe what I believe?

A son once told his father that he was being bullied at primary school. 'What can I do, Dad?' he asked. Being a good Christian man the father said, 'Next time this kid does this to you, hit him! Make sure you hit him hard enough so that he's not going to get up. Just finish it there and then.' (He was leaning on his experience.)

After a few days the boy came back and said, 'Dad, it worked. It's all fine now.' The father asked if he had got into any trouble with his teachers, but he said no. About a year or so later he confessed, 'I'm having the same problems at school again, Dad.' 'Right, well, you know what to do,' he was told. 'Clobber this lad, and it's all going to be fine again.'

A few days later the father asked him how things were at school. He said, 'I thought about what you said and then I read in *Topz*[6] that if you've got difficulties with someone you should pray for them. So I started praying, and now he's my friend.'

Our human filters don't always give us the right answer. We need to develop a biblical world-view in order to work out what our responses and reactions should be.

THE BIG TRUTH

It's not always easy to know exactly what the truth is. Our perceptions can colour how we see things. Have you ever seen those picture puzzles that combine two or more images? Which image we naturally see when we look depends on our perception.

We all see the world differently. When you see an image of a rug, do you see a floor covering, a souvenir or a place of prayer?

There are many different perceptions of life. Have you ever wondered how you came to your particular one? Or are you just unthinkingly carried along by it? An un-churched teenager once described her world-view in one bleak sentence: 'You're born today, you're dead tomorrow and you live in between.' If I believed that, my life wouldn't be worth living. But that is a world-view that so many people cope with, day in, day out.

Our world-view will influence our perception of God. How has your image of God been formed and developed in your life? As a young child how did you view God, and how has that image of God changed since? Or, has it remained the same? Then, how might this affect your response to questions such as: What is the nature of human beings? What is the purpose of humankind? What does freedom mean to you? How do you know what you know? How do you know it's true? How do you know your view is correct?

When I first started counselling training I went to a huge library where there were hundreds of different books and hundreds of different approaches to life. Each one thought theirs was the best and right approach. It can be confusing, can't it? Who's got the best approach? How can we tell? But nearly all of these resources agree on the factors that influence the way in which our world-view is formed.

I. EXPERIENCE

Each one of us has unique experiences of the world around us that make up our view of what the world means. The way we are treated by others, the culture in which we are brought up and the way we process what has happened to us all play a part in forming our views.

2. EDUCATION

Some of us have highly-developed thought processes that have influenced our world-view, and many of these are born out of what we learn in books, on the internet or from our teachers. Negative and positive lessons about ourselves and the world around us can find their anchor point in our educative background.

3. OBSERVATION

Watching the way other people handle situations and speak about their problems or lives is another way we can develop our view of the world. But, of course, we can only ever observe what people *choose* to show us. (This is in part why the media is so very influential.)

These are all very interesting ways to look at life, of course, but they are also incredibly flawed. They result in a secular world-view that leads us to travel in concentric circles. God's desire for us is that we develop a biblical world-view, His world-view. After all, it is His design!

THE BIG ASK

So, let's get down to nitty-gritty. How do we do this? How do we get God's perspective? Perhaps we could start by considering how *not* to do it!

Our world looks for wisdom in the following three-part process:

1. We seek knowledge.
2. Then we gain understanding.
3. As a result, we ultimately gain wisdom.

On the face of it, this sounds quite sensible. But actually the Bible asks us to gain wisdom from God first. Read this beautiful passage from

Proverbs 2:1–8 from *The Message* version of the Bible, and you will see what I mean:

> Good friend, take to heart what I'm telling you;
>   collect my counsels and guard them with your life.
> Tune your ears to the world of Wisdom;
>   set your heart on a life of Understanding.
> That's right – if you make Insight your priority,
>   and won't take no for an answer,
> Searching for it like a prospector panning for gold,
>   like an adventurer on a treasure hunt,
> Believe me, before you know it Fear-of-God will be yours;
>   you'll have come upon the Knowledge of God.
>
> And here's why: God gives out Wisdom free,
>   is plainspoken in Knowledge and Understanding.
> He's a rich mine of Common Sense for those who live well,
>   a personal bodyguard to the candid and sincere.
> He keeps his eye on all who live honestly,
>   and pays special attention to his loyally committed ones.

I love the fact that God gives out wisdom like this. We become wise through His revelations to us. Maybe today it's time to start listening to a new voice. God longs to speak to us, not just through His Word but through His world, too.

CHAPTER 3

THE
GOOD
life

> 'Real holiness has love for its essence, humility for its clothing, the good of others for its employment, and the honour of God as its end.'

NATHANIEL EMMONS

03

GOOD

In the forests of northern Europe and Asia lives a little animal called an Ermine. Known for its snow-white fur in winter, it instinctively protects its white coat against anything that would soil it. Fur hunters take advantage of this unusual trait of the Ermine. They don't set a snare to catch them, but instead they find the Ermine's home, which is usually a cleft in a rock or a hollow in an old tree. They smear the entrance and interior with grime. Then the hunters set their dogs loose to find and chase the Ermine. The frightened animal flees toward home but doesn't enter because of the filth outside. Rather than soil its white coat, the creature is trapped by the dogs and captured while preserving its purity. For the Ermine, purity is more precious than life.

H.G. Bosch[1]

WHAT IS HOLINESS?

Holiness is one of those words that can be hard to satisfactorily define. The very sound of the word can be intimidating, can't it? People sometimes even use the word 'holy' for another Christian who they don't get on with very well. Describing someone as being a bit 'holy' can be shorthand for saying, 'They are not part of *my* circle of friends.' In other words, they come across as a bit 'holier than thou' – a negative term for someone who is pious, but who displays little genuine humanity.

Often when people hear the word 'holy' it can elicit feelings of guilt – that we don't measure up. To be holy is often seen as an impossible duty rather than a joy or a privilege. It can conjure up images of stern-faced people with big black Bibles who have forgotten how to have fun. The media often portrays holiness as a form of two-faced hypocrisy. A well-known UK TV soap once featured a character who was a fiery Pentecostal preacher, but also secretly a serial murderer. Christianity is sadly misrepresented and it is partly our fault. I think we have allowed others to continue misunderstanding what it really means to be holy – to live a life less ordinary.

The Bible talks about holiness in very different terms. Look how Peter puts it:

 … you are a chosen people, a royal priesthood, a holy nation, a people belonging to God.

1 Pet. 2:9

This doesn't strike me as at all negative or impossible to achieve. We are a people who are chosen, royal, holy and belonging to God. Surely that's something to get very excited about? Peter is saying that holiness is part of our identity as Christians. It is not something we need to fight for (or against).

So what do we really mean by holiness and, more importantly, what does God mean? My very simple definition, but one which is, I hope, helpful to you is this: being holy is *living as God intended*. There is a profound simplicity to biblical holiness that is positively releasing. Holiness is about *being* and *having* all God intended for us.

Some people inevitably view holiness as restrictive and constrictive, feeling constrained by boundaries in life and they react against them. But the truth is, God's boundaries – His guidelines for successful living – are not given to crush or imprison us, but to set us free. When we know where the boundaries are, we can roam free. Fences put up along the perimeter of a cliff are not there to spoil our fun. Similarly, God's boundaries are protective measures put in place by our loving, heavenly Father. Consequences to living outside these boundaries can be far-reaching, with long-term impact to many. Take this scenario for example: a young man 'sleeps around', rejecting such boundaries, his girlfriend gets pregnant and, even though they don't really love each other, they get married – the marriage doesn't last and so it goes on – there is much pain and distress caused, with a child, or perhaps children, now involved and affected too.

God says that certain things are out of bounds for us because He knows that our actions have consequences, and all kinds of unwanted results can occur.

Moving towards a God-intended, God-designed life means maturing in Christ, and this is not possible without holiness. Let's examine further what this means for us.

HOLINESS IS SEPARATION, BUT NOT ISOLATION

A common word for holy in the Bible means to be 'separate'. But separate from what? One difficulty among believers is that they often take the issue of separation too literally. They separate themselves from people, from their culture, and strive to live in some kind of Christian bubble, protected from the influence of the world at large. They are more than separated, they are *isolated*. This is not what holiness is about. The beautiful truth of God's holiness is that He did not require separation from others to be holy. In fact, the incarnation of Christ is our clearest example of His holiness. Jesus, the Holy One, was separated entirely for God's purposes, but He chose to live in close proximity with the world.

He was known as the friend of sinners and yet He was still holy.

When, through sin, human beings created a wall of separation between themselves and God, God chose not to stay separate. He took on skin and bones and maintained His holiness as He walked around in the dust of the earth. Living in God's holiness, therefore, is not about separating ourselves from the world, but about immersing ourselves in the world to demonstrate His love. We don't need to either mimic the world's standards or lifestyle, or dilute or change our message, but we are to live fully in the world – to effectively live out and demonstrate the love of God.

I don't want to be part of a separatist Church that withdraws and becomes irrelevant, misunderstood and marginalised. I want to align myself with the incarnational God. Read Paul's inspirational perspective on the subject in Romans 12:1–2:

> So here's what I want you to do, God helping you: Take your everyday, ordinary life – your sleeping, eating, going-to-work, and walking-around life – and place it before God as an offering. Embracing what God does for you is the best thing you can do for him. Don't become so well-adjusted to your culture that you fit into it without even thinking. Instead, fix your attention on God. You'll be changed from the inside out. Readily recognise what he wants from you, and quickly respond to it. Unlike the culture around you, always dragging you down to its level of immaturity, God brings the best out of you, develops well-formed maturity in you.
>
> *The Message*

Like Paul, I want to 'embrace what God does' for me and keep on being transformed from the inside out. John Eldredge talks about holiness in terms of our sensitivity to God as opposed to numbness to Him. He says that our problem is that we have grown accustomed to seeking God in other things.[2] We need to recapture our sensitivity.

HOLINESS IS BEING LIKE GOD

Throughout Church history, people have been of one mind on the reason for living a holy life. Leviticus 19:2 says:

> 'Speak to the entire assembly of Israel and say to them:
> "Be holy because I, the LORD your God, am holy."'

God's desire for you and for me is that we become people after His heart and His character. When we become Christians, God implants in each of us the yearning to know Him better and more deeply by becoming more like Him. But much depends on whether we choose to cultivate this desire or simply ignore it.

The prophet Isaiah speaks of this most powerfully:

> 'Woe to me!' I cried. 'I am ruined! For I am a man of unclean lips, and I live among a people of unclean lips, and my eyes have seen the King, the LORD Almighty.' Then one of the seraphs flew to me with a live coal in his hand, which he had taken with tongs from the altar. With it he touched my mouth and said, 'See, this has touched your lips; your guilt is taken away and your sin atoned for.'
>
> Isa. 6:5–7

The blinding glimpse that he experiences of God's holiness fills him with a desire to be holy too. A live coal touches his lips and he is made clean and pure and is then able to do what God is asking of him.

Remember, also, the story of Jesus in the boat with Peter, when He asks Peter to let down his nets again for a catch:

> When they had done so, they caught such a large number of fish that their nets began to break. So they signalled to their partners in the other boat to come and help them, and they came and filled both boats so full that they began to sink. When Simon Peter saw this, he fell at Jesus' knees and said, 'Go away from me, Lord; I am a sinful man!'
>
> Luke 5:6–8

Notice Peter's reaction to the awesome demonstration of God's power. Again, like Isaiah, he realises his own ungodliness and sin. This same desire to be rid of sin and to pursue a holy lifestyle is characteristic of all those who long for a close relationship with God. Holiness is the first thing that the Holy Spirit wants to impart to us as we set out on our personal spiritual journey – the journey of walking more closely with God.

John Stott wrote, 'One of the God-appointed functions of the Holy Spirit is to make us know, feel, mourn, loath, and forsake our sins.'[3] It is evident that we are walking in holiness when we are no longer comfortable with sin. Sin becomes less attractive as we grow more attracted to God's ways, purposes and plans for us.

As Christians, our primary calling on the earth, whatever our own subgoals, aims and gifting might be, is to be Christ's ambassadors, God's representatives. In order to carry out this mandate effectively it helps to be like Him! Otherwise we are misrepresenting Him and all He stands for. I have to say that after walking with Christ for a number of years and having been a husband, a father, a friend, a counsellor, a minister and a people-helper, the way God goes about producing His image in me is through making me more holy.

A.W. Tozer eloquently described the holiness that God possesses and that He wants to bestow on us:

> Holy is the way God is. To be holy, He does not conform to a standard. He is that standard. He is absolutely holy with an infinite, incomprehensible fullness of purity that is incapable of being other than it is. Because He is holy, all His attributes are holy; that is, whatever we think of as belonging to God must be thought of as holy.[4]

And as we saw in Chapter 1 the apostle Paul summed up God's intentions perfectly in Romans 8:29–30:

> God knew what he was doing from the very beginning. He decided from the outset to shape the lives of those who love him along the same lines as the life of his Son. The Son stands first in the line of humanity he restored. We see the original and intended shape of our lives there in him. After God made that decision of what his children should be like, he followed it up by calling people by name. After he called them by name, he set them on a solid basis with himself. And then, after getting them established, he stayed with them to the end, gloriously completing what he had begun.
>
> *The Message*

Thought of in these terms, the words of God to 'Be holy because I, the LORD your God, am holy' (Lev. 19:2) read much more like a benediction God speaks over us than a harshly spoken command that demands our compliance.

I am so glad that God is at work in my life in this way. God is so pleased and excited about Jesus that He wants to make me and you like Him! And it is through the process of our spiritual formation that God goes about the task of producing the image of Christ in us. I'm discovering that, actually, the best way to understand holiness is not to seek a definition, but to seek the divine.

Have you noticed that when people spend time together they start to become like one another? Husbands and wives use similar vocabulary and speech patterns, young people dress alike or share similar interests. So it is with spending time with Jesus. The more time we spend in His company, the more we will begin to reflect His holy nature.

HOLINESS IS A JOURNEY

Sadly, there has been a tendency amongst Christians to believe that being holy is some kind of one-off commitment; that it comes as standard when we are saved. But I have found that holiness is not like that at all. It is a journey – a process that takes an entire lifetime to complete.

Holiness is also not necessarily about just 'being good' or sticking to the rules. As Christians we are people who adhere to far more than just a rigid code of conduct. We are people who are made pure as a result of proximity to God. That's how we become holy. When we walk with Him daily and we open the details of our lives to Him, it produces an authentic purity.

The writer to the Hebrews exhorted us to

> Follow peace with all men, and holiness, without which no one will see the Lord.
>
> Heb. 12:14, AV

I don't know about you, but I want to see the Lord! I want to be made more like Him each day. But, you have no doubt found, like me, that many things get in your way and hinder this process. Many of us simply fill our lives with service, and we get far too busy. It's easy to become so focused on exuberant beginnings and victorious endings that we forget the important matter of living well in between. Sometimes we fail and feel like giving up. But part of maturing in Christ is about becoming what Paul describes in Romans 6:18 as 'slaves to righteousness'. Fundamentally, we are holy because God has made us so. There is no holiness in us without Him – it's not something we can do. He does it for us.

HOLINESS IS TRUE HEALTH

Holiness is also about wholeness. I find this both really encouraging and incredibly challenging. Holiness is not just the absence of sin, but also the presence of health and wholeness in our lives. When we fail God we are not reflecting His character or behaving as whole people. Instead, we are contradicting ourselves and denying the identity we have been given to possess. Part of the Anglican liturgy includes these helpful words:

> We have done the things we ought not to have done, and left undone the things we ought to have done, and there is no health in us.
>
> *The Book of Common Prayer*

Thomas Carlyle writes:

> The old word for holy in the German language, 'heilig', also means healthy ... You could not get any better definition of what holy really is than healthy – completely healthy.[5]

Our holiness, our wellbeing and even our health are compromised just as much when we fail to do good as when we do what's wrong.

To explain it another way, holiness is about walking towards what is right, not just walking away from sin.

HOLINESS IS ACTIVE, NOT PASSIVE

Jesus speaks clearly about what our lives should be like. Notice how His language is intentional and proactive:

> 'You are the light of the world ... let your light shine before men, that they may see your good deeds and praise your Father in heaven.'
>
> Matt. 5:14–16

He described Himself very similarly as the 'light of the world' (John 8:12). Like Jesus, we are not meant to live lives with a light that simply avoids being extinguished, but rather to illuminate the darkest recesses of the globe. Being holy is about being visible, about being able to light the path for others and show them how to live. What it means for us to be holy is not just resisting being pulled down by the world, but pulling the world up with us as we reflect the love of God.

But holiness is not purely about what we do. Indeed, if we tried to make it so we would end up with nothing more than sweaty self-effort and frustration! We can't maintain the goodness on our own. Co-operating with the Holy Spirit is how real change happens. As James H. Aughey said, 'Holiness is not the way to Christ; Christ is the way to holiness.' And whenever contradictory messages in our culture scream at us, here is the truth: *the godly life is an exciting life.* Jesus is the way, the truth and the life. It is He who enables us to be holy. He is God, Emmanuel, the One who is with us and in us on our amazing and exhilarating quest to be holy.

HOLINESS IS ATTAINABLE

When people talk about holiness it reminds me of the person who prayed a certain prayer. Maybe you've heard it before?

> Dear God, so far today I've done all right. I haven't gossiped, I haven't lost my temper, I haven't been greedy, grumpy, selfish or over-indulgent and I'm very thankful to you for that. But in a few minutes I'll have to get out of bed and from then on I'm probably going to need a lot more help!

It is tempting to view holiness as something that is utterly unobtainable. But it is not. Have a look at this amazing truth from Exodus 31:13 where God, speaking through Moses, says,

> 'Say to the Israelites, "You must observe my Sabbaths. This will be a sign between me and you for the generations to come, so you may know that I am the LORD, who makes you holy."'

It is God who not only desires our holiness, but who helps us to become holy.

The early saints discovered that their holiness didn't arise out of the things they did – it came from the One they were doing them for. Holiness rubbed off on them because they spent a lot of time in the presence of Jesus. Spending time in God's presence is the way to living a life less ordinary, a life of holiness. It's an invitation from a Holy God to be with Him and become like Him.

A HOLY LIFE IS HOLISTIC

I meet a lot of Christians who are on the path to maturity in some areas of their lives. They may be incredible Bible teachers or fabulous intercessors, but in other areas they are terribly underdeveloped. Perhaps they know their Bibles really well, but relationally they are incredibly poor; their words come over as harsh and unremitting. I have known people who spent hours in prayer, but within two minutes of starting a conversation would say something completely unhelpful to someone. Holiness can never be about just one aspect of our lives.

Holiness is holistic – it encompasses all of life. We cannot separate the spiritual from the secular. Jesus never spoke about having a good 'spiritual life', just about living a good life. In the Hebrew language there is no word for 'spiritual'. God wants to be part of every aspect of our lives. As Rob Bell commented, 'To label one part of your life "spiritual" is to label other parts "unspiritual". It is absolutely foreign to the worldview of Jesus.'[6]

Holiness isn't a sticking plaster for our sin. It's not about Sunday morning posturing. It's about a renewed life, a renewed mind and a renewed lifestyle. Nathanael Emmons, an American theologian of a few centuries ago said, 'Holiness has love for its essence, humility for its clothing, the good of others as its employment, and the honour of God as its end.'

A HOLY LIFE IS TRANSFORMATIONAL

Holiness, then, is not about self-actualisation – becoming all that *we* want to be – but is a daily process of *God-transformation*. It is, as Dallas Willard described, a 'total renovation of the heart.'[7] But there is nothing instant about it, lest we think this can happen overnight.

Scott Peck, in his book *The Road Less Traveled*,[8] describes those who want to grow but don't have the time or the energy for it. There are many people who possess a vision for personal development, but seem to lack the will for it. Instead they want to find an easy shortcut to sainthood. We (and this is so me!) see what we want to do, and just want to take the shortcut. Often people will attempt to attain it by superficially imitating the holiness they see in others. Sometimes we just pretend, don't we? We say all the right things and look the part, but inside we are not there at all. Scott Peck goes on to say:

> Some even believe that by such imitation they have really become saints and prophets and they are unable to acknowledge that they are still children and face the painful fact they must start at the beginning and go through the middle.

I'm not for one minute suggesting that you are like this, but some of us suffer from a peculiar Christian phenomenon I like to call 'home group rush'. If you run a home/cell/house group, you may know what I am talking about. Five minutes before people are due to arrive, someone is running around with a Hoover, someone else is chucking dirty dishes in a cupboard whilst yelling at the kids to get in the bath, and someone else is locking the dog outside. In short, chaos! Then the doorbell rings and a sudden and deliberate 'calm' descends on the house. Visitors to the house inwardly chastise themselves and feel like failures because all they see is the sparklingly clean kitchen and the equally clean children. Pleasantries are exchanged, but they sit down thinking, 'This house is so beautiful. My life is not like this!' If only they had been there two minutes earlier!

Being holy is not about being perfect. It is not about having a set of totally unrealistic legalistic 'attainments'. That can only lead to pride or, worse, to despair. Holiness is about gazing on Jesus Christ and His perfection. We need to give each other a break sometimes on our journey towards holy living. We need to know that, actually, it's OK to fail – to fall flat on our faces, but then get up, dust ourselves off and begin walking again. We need to allow people to be normal and, when they make mistakes, to recover from them, receive our encouragement and continue journeying.

The Archbishop of Canterbury, Rowan Williams, said,

> A human being is holy, not because he or she triumphs by willpower over chaos and guilt and leads a flawless life, but because that life shows the victory of God's faithfulness in the midst of disorder and imperfection. The church is holy ... not because it is a gathering of the good and the well-behaved, but because it speaks of the triumph of grace in the coming together of strangers and sinners who, miraculously, trust one another enough to join in common repentance and common praise ... Humanly speaking, holiness is always like this: God's endurance in the midst of our refusal of him, his capacity to meet every refusal with the gift of himself.[9]

HOLINESS IS RELATIONAL

Like God, holy people will express their holiness in the way they relate to others – hence the call to demonstrate our love for God in the way that we love those around us. If being holy doesn't make us more loving and kind, then I would really question whether we are making any progress at all. Holy living is what we were born for.

There is a fascinating book called *In the Land of the Believers* that tells of how Gina Welch, an atheist journalist, went undercover amongst evangelical Christians in one of the southern states of America to find out what they were really like. Her story is compelling, but sad.

> I put on ugly buckle loafers, a loose purple sweater and
> joined ... Baptist Church. I had to grow out my short hair
> and put on some weight – which I called my temporary
> church body and I replaced my gold nail polish with 'good
> girl pink'.[10]

She said the dowdiness was strategic – she was trying to look
'evangelical'. (Is this how we have allowed those outside the Church
to see and understand us?) 'I wanted to know what my evangelical
neighbours were like', she writes. 'Christians have violently side-
parted hair, buckle their belts under ponderous bellies, think
aeroplane travel is exotic and leave lousy tips.' She goes on to say
how she didn't fit in, but tried to do all the right things. She makes
statements such as, 'I got baptised, but the water was cold and it made
my mascara run'.

Reading this and numerous other descriptions, I can't help but
think she was assessing the Christians around her purely on a
behavioural level. She was examining the superficial, cultural aspects
of Christianity expressed in one place in the world. But she wasn't
getting under the skin and personality of Jesus; she was simply
caught up with the outward appearance, trappings and traditions
of His followers. This is the same error made by the Pharisees. They
were more concerned with how things appeared than what was really
taking place inside. Their pious behaviour masked the unchanged
attitudes of greed and pride in their lives.

At the end of the Second World War, the battle cruiser the *USS
Indianapolis* was making its way across the Pacific when it was
torpedoed by a Japanese submarine. It sank within minutes and
300 of the 1,200 men died. The remaining 900 men went into the
sea. After four days and five nights without fresh water, only 316 of
these men survived. The medical officers, who knew of its dangers,

had called out and pleaded with the men not to drink the salty sea water. But many of them were so thirsty that they ignored the desperate warnings.

Holiness is similar to this. Because we are relational beings, we look around us to see what others are doing. Having assessed the situation, we often then feel comfortable fitting in with, and doing, what the majority are doing. We 'drink' the same water as the rest of society, and end up suffering from the same afflictions. Holiness is about following Jesus not the crowd, and not looking for immediate comfort. Instead we need to align ourselves with something lasting and pure and wait until we hear, see and taste something of God.

The author Anne Rice, who rose to fame for her novels about vampires, originally left the Church as a young person, but returned in recent years, publishing a book in 2008 entitled *Called Out of Darkness: A Spiritual Confession*. Sadly, she later told the Associated Press that she had become increasingly dissatisfied with the Church over child abuse scandals and its reaction to the crisis, as well as the excommunication of a nun, Sister Margaret McBride, who approved an abortion for a woman whose health was in jeopardy. Describing the Church, Rice said, 'It's simply impossible for me to "belong" to this quarrelsome, hostile, disputatious and deservedly infamous group. For ten years, I've tried. I've failed. I'm an outsider. My conscience will allow nothing else.' She went on to say:

> My commitment to God is as firm as ever. I want to keep that commitment front and centre in my life, but I have to walk away from the churches. The anger and frustration becomes so toxic you have to conclude that this is coming between me and God. I can't let that happen. I can't follow His followers.[11]

Rice later elaborated on her position by writing this statement: 'My faith in Christ is central to my life. My conversion from a pessimistic atheist lost in a world I didn't understand, to an optimistic believer in a universe created and sustained by a loving God is crucial to me.'[12]

Rice felt that following Christ was something she could handle, but not walking alongside His people. This is an all too familiar story. Her scathing words about the Church are harsh, but there is truth in them. We can get so caught up with doing rather than being that we lose all perspective on life. We can work too hard on adhering to laws, and not pay any attention to love. I am not saying we shouldn't 'do', I'm just saying that our doing should come out of our being. Holiness is about who we belong to and who we are.

GOD'S BREAKTHROUGH

We don't have to be overwhelmed by what's ahead on our journey into holiness, however. Be encouraged, because God has broken into our lives with His outrageous and amazing grace.

Philip Greenslade relates this true story:

> On the 22 November 1963, the playwright David Lodge was in a theatre watching one of his creations being performed on stage. In the middle of the play a character was scripted to turn on a radio and look for a local station. On this particular day the theatre was absolutely full and the actors were caught up in the drama of their performance. The character took the radio, flicked it and turned the tuning dial. Suddenly a voice broke through, 'Today in Dallas, President Kennedy was killed.' The actor tried to turn the radio off, but the real world had burst into the make-believe

world. People just left. No one wanted to see a pretend play any more. Real life was more compelling and urgent.[13]

Sometimes God gives us a 'wake-up call' like this. He breaks into our lives with His character and His purposes, and takes our attention away from the stage of the world. We need this. We all, at times, feel discouraged and overwhelmed, but let me encourage you to persevere. Becoming holy is a messy business that requires time and dedication. Very often for me it feels like one step forward and two steps back. Some days are better than others. But even on my bad days, I am aware that some of my greatest leaps of maturity have been made possible by the platform of my failures.

We need to remember that holy living is not something that we do alone. The Bible describes us as the saints of God. You are a saint, whether you see yourself as one or not. Sainthood is not a title conferred on special people who live perfectly and can perform miracles! Sainthood is about being set apart for the purpose of God. Being a saint is a team task. God has always sought to use not just individuals, but communities. So as we commit ourselves to the joys and pains of being together we can become a lighthouse that gives brightness to our communities. As D.L. Moody once said, 'A holy life will make the deepest impression. Lighthouses blow no horns, they just shine.'

life
T⊕GETHER

*'Friendship is born at that moment
when one person says to another,
"What! You too? I thought
I was the only one."'*

C.S. LEWIS[1]

EVERYTHING IS ABOUT RELATING

From the opening to the closing pages of the Bible, the overwhelming message of Scripture is one of *relationship*. In the very first phrase we meet a deeply relational God. Those four little words 'In the beginning God' in Genesis 1:1 are pungent with meaning. The word used here for 'God' comes not from a singlar but a plural word, *Elohim*. This does not mean 'gods' plural, but God in His three-part form. Later, in Genesis 1:26, we read a plural word again, 'Let us make man in *our* image' (italics mine), when God speaks out the directive for the creation of humankind to His Son and to His Spirit. So it is that we encounter a God who is so deeply invested in the principle of relationship that He embodies it within His very being.

As Larry Crabb puts it:

> If one believes that God exists as three persons, who are distinct enough to actually relate to one another, then it becomes clear somehow that the final nature of things is wrapped up in the idea of relationship ... God is a personal being who exists eternally in a relationship among persons. He is His own community.[2]

In His teaching Jesus highlighted *relationships*, both vertical and horizontal, as occupying the pinnacle of God's commandments:

... an expert in the law, tested him with this question: 'Teacher, which is the greatest commandment in the Law?' Jesus replied: '"Love the Lord your God with all your heart and with all your soul and with all your mind." This is the first and greatest commandment. And the second is like it: "Love your neighbour as yourself." All the Law and the Prophets hang on these two commandments.'

Matt. 22:35–40

Jesus maintained that our primary function and calling in life is to be in *relationship* with God, and to love Him with all that we are. The 'overflow' of that calling is to love others, showing them the same kind of deference, honour and respect we normally reserve for ourselves. Many of us find this mandate challenging – especially since most of us know a few people who are far easier to love from a distance!

SOCIETY STRUGGLES TO BE RELATIONAL

It is a fact that we live in a society where relationships are complex and messy, and breakdowns in marriages and families are commonplace. Today many children have multiple parents and step-siblings, and tensions can run high within and between blended familes. In general, our society has undergone a massive shift in perspective as far as relationships are concerned. A community focus, where people looked out for and looked after one another, has steadily given way to an individual focus, where everything revolves around 'me' and 'my needs' – an 'I' generation. People now readily pursue their own happiness and wellbeing at the expense of others. The needs of the individual have been exalted over the wider needs of community – and the change in perspective has been telling.

But still, every person, regardless of their circumstances, education or background, longs for relationships of meaning and significance. However dysfunctional our start in life, we still find ourselves searching for the right kind of relationship. We all want to matter to someone else – and we show this in many different ways. Why are relationships so important to us? Because to be in relationship was part of our original design, and is a key way in which we experience significance. Each of us is looking for ways in which we can be affirmed and increase our self-worth, the success of which depends significantly on the way in which we relate to God, ourselves and others.

In all of this, we must realise that the way in which the people of God respond to the needs of our changed and changing world is really crucial. So how do we do it?

We first need to reconnect with the heart of the Father, understanding that relationship and community lie at the very heart of who He is and what His plan for creation is all about. Living in constant, healthy relationship in the 'family' of His Son and His Spirit, Father God models for us the type of co-dependent relationship that we need to emulate. He does not intend for humanity to live lives that support individualism, but to live and love in close-knit, mutually beneficial, other-centred relationships. Then, secure in the knowledge of God's love and acceptance of us, we can make ourselves vulnerable to love others in a truly relational way.

GOD'S PLAN FOR US IS RELATIONAL

The Bible tells us that we are all made 'in the image' (Gen. 1:27) of God. Of course, that doesn't mean we have the shape of His face or the same colour hair. Primarily, it means that just like Him we are made to relate to those around us. When God said, 'It is not good for the man to be alone. I will make a helper suitable for him' (Gen. 2:18), I don't think He was simply talking about marriage! Just as relationship is an integral part of the Trinity, so it plays a vital role in what it means to be fully human. I need you and you need me. How else can I see what God looks like, unless I have you to demonstrate Him to me?

When God called Abraham He said he would make His descendants as numerous as the stars in the sky. Moses was promised that God would make a great nation out of those he was leading to the promised land. God's call was and is not just about individuals, but about communities. It is about showing His blessing to whole nations.

When Jesus was on earth and about to begin His ministry, what was the first thing He did? He called others to share the experience with Him.

Significance, self-worth and security are what we long for. The trouble is that we often look for those things in human relationships first. We may find it for a time, but ultimately we will fail to find a perfect person who meets our every need in a consistent way. True friendship and relationship with others has got to come from a place not of *need*, but of security in our relationship with God. To that end we need to ask God to give us His perspective on who we are and what we mean to Him. Only when we know who we are in Christ (and what we are not) can we truly function as those who maintain healthy relationships with others.

We are secure when we feel accepted and loved unconditionally. If any relationship is fully secure it gives us peace, takes away the fear of rejection, and allows us to feel safe enough to fail as well as succeed. Dr E. Stanley Jones in his definition of relationship said, 'We are only as mature as our relationships.' How true this is.

THE ART OF MAKING GOOD RELATIONSHIPS

If we are to become people who are committed to good relationships, there are a few patterns and habits we can develop that will help us. Numbers of books are filled with good practices and techniques we can learn and develop, but in this short section let's consider certain qualities that should characterise who we are.

We need to be:

PEOPLE OF VALUE

Joann C. Jones made this interesting observation about valuing others:

> During my second year of nursing school our professor gave us a quiz. I breezed through the questions until I read the last one: 'What is the first name of the woman who cleans the school?' Surely this was a joke. I had seen the cleaning woman several times, but how would I know her name? I handed in my paper, leaving the last question blank. Before the class ended, one student asked if the last question would count towards our grade. 'Absolutely,' the professor said. 'In your careers, you will meet many people. All are significant. They deserve your attention and care, even if all you do is smile and say hello.' I've never forgotten that lesson. I also learned her name was Dorothy.[3]

We can be those who show others what they mean to us. Not just that we appreciate what they are good at and what they can *do*, but who they *are*. In Ephesians 2:10, Paul describes us collectively, saying, 'For we are God's workmanship'. He chooses his words carefully. He could have used the word *erga* to describe the fact that God made us, meaning the daily grind or labour of any kind. Instead he used the word *poièma*, meaning a highly creative, thoughtful piece of work wrought by a craftsman. The New Living Translation of the Bible captures Paul's meaning well, translating this phrase as 'we are God's masterpiece'. These words are highly revealing about the way in which God views His creation, and particularly us as individuals. Masterpieces come in all shapes, sizes and styles, but share one thing in common – they are highly valuable. So we are all different, but of great worth to God. Truly understanding this for ourselves will have an impact on the way we treat those around us.

PE⊕PLE ⊕F PEACE

An unknown author once wrote, 'Don't let people drive you crazy when you know it's in walking distance!' We all have things that annoy and frustrate us about others. None of us are perfect when it comes to getting along with those who are different from us, are we? There always seem to be people whose sole purpose in life is to teach us how to be patient and how to master the art of biting our tongue! It is certainly true that people can *blister us* or *bless us*.

Nevertheless, the Bible is clear that we should be those who seek peace at all times.

Titus 3:1–2 says:

> … be ready to do whatever is good, to slander no-one, to
> be peaceable and considerate, and to show true humility
> towards all men.

It's a classic saying that the world would be perfect if it weren't for people – just like the Church would be a perfect place if I weren't there! Wherever people group together in some kind of large organisation, there will be tension and clashes of personality, and the

Church is not immune from this. It is a fact of life that certain people will find it difficult to get along with other people. All sorts of minor jealousies and quarrels can come to the surface when imperfect people are around.

I believe it was Dr E. Stanley Jones who defined Christianity as, 'The science of relating well to others in the Spirit of Jesus Christ'. The issue of personal, peaceful relationships is of vital importance. We are good at so many things in the Church – worship music, preaching, creating conferences, setting up community programmes – but sometimes we really struggle to model the simple things.

Keeping in mind that God desires us to be at peace with one another will help. We need to work proactively to be a people who don't just try to keep the peace, but make it.

PEOPLE OF GRACE AND FORGIVENESS

Over the years, I've met so many people who have been hurt by relationships that have gone wrong. It's tempting to focus here on the 'big ones' like marriage breakdown and divorce, but the truth is we can be wounded emotionally by all manner of minor skirmishes: bullying, competitiveness, jealousy, anger, inferiority, fear, and many more besides. Human beings have a terrible habit of having a hit and run mentality to relationships – sometimes knowingly and sadly sometimes completely unaware!

I've met many Christians who have been hurt by other Christians. The term 'friendly fire' is one we hear a lot these days in news bulletins – a euphemism to describe the death of a member of the armed forces at the hands of their own side. Often we can be guilty of inflicting 'friendly fire' on other Christians. We can play mind games, manipulate people, or damage them by how we treat or speak about them.

King David knew about the kind of pain this causes. In Psalm 41:9 he lamented, 'Even my close friend, whom I trusted, he who shared my bread, has lifted up his heel against me'. You can feel the rejection, hurt and betrayal in his words. Jesus Himself echoed these words in John 13:18: 'He who shares my bread has lifted up his heel against me.'

The way we treat people reveals a lot about us. There is a lot of truth in the saying, 'Hurt people hurt people.' Some people live by the precept Ernest Hemmingway aptly described when he said, 'We have to distrust each other. It's our only defence against betrayal.' Most of us would not consciously admit to living like this, but if we were to look deeper, we might be surprised to learn just how much we guard our emotions, erecting barriers of protection against potential hurt. We are frequently closed, and suspicious of others. We find it hard to trust people. Yet, God wants us to live lives that express grace and forgiveness. He wants our lives to be characterised by those traits we see in Jesus.

How do people feel about you? What do people say when you leave a meeting? Are you known as someone who lights up the room or someone who lives under a cloud? The way we treat others is catching. The root word for influenza or flu is also the root of the word 'influence'. You and I have an influence on our churches, home groups, neighbourhoods, places of work, schools and families, for good or for ill.

So what kind of influencer are you? In *The Friendship Book*, author Francis Gay relates this thought-provoking tale:

> As the bus slowed down at the crowded bus stop, the bus conductor leaned from the platform and called out, 'Six only!' The bus stopped. He counted on six passengers, rang the bell, and then, as the bus moved off, called to those left behind: 'So sorry, plenty of room in my heart – but the bus is full!' He left behind a row of smiling faces. It's not what you do, it's the way that you do it.[4]

There is an ancient Chinese proverb that says, 'A bit of fragrance always clings to the hand that gives roses'. Let's aim to be people who leave a sweet fragrance behind when others encounter us.

PEOPLE OF LOVE AND HOPE

Mary Kay Ash wrote that 'As aerodynamic engineers "proved" many years ago, the bumblebee cannot fly! Its wings are too weak, and its body is too heavy. Fortunately, the bumblebee doesn't know that and goes right on flying.'[5] God hasn't called us to live in a limited way. Like the bumblebee, we are capable of 'flying' and doing far more as a Christian than we could ever have imagined before we met and trusted Jesus. One aspect of this is that God enables us to love people in ways we never thought possible, and to possess a hope that prevails against all odds.

God hasn't called us to live in distrust or fear, but to be people of trust and hope. When I first became a Christian, I read the prayer in the back of the booklet *Journey Into Life* and, just as I finished praying the prayer, which I meant with all my heart, a thought dropped into my mind. 'I'm going to have to go to church and mix with all those people!' I immediately started to backtrack. I wanted to know God, but I wasn't sure about a whole church full of His people.

Since then, however, I have discovered some amazing people in the churches I've been blessed to be a part of. Some of those 'odd' people became my closest friends! They were and still are like family to me. In fact, I am eternally indebted to those people who stood by me and believed in me, particularly in the earliest days of my walk as a Christian, as I took my first faltering steps.

One of the most famous passages in the Bible, 1 Corinthians 13:4–8, illustrates this unique brand of love and hope in action:

> Love is patient, love is kind. It does not envy, it does not
> boast, it is not proud. It is not rude, it is not self-seeking,

it is not easily angered, it keeps no record of wrongs. Love does not delight in evil but rejoices with the truth. It always protects, always trusts, always hopes, always perseveres. Love never fails.

It is this kind of loving and 'hopefulness' I was shown and exposed to as a new Christian. This is what needs to characterise our relationships with those God has put around us.

PE⊕PLE ⊕F PRESENCE

Gordon Fee says:

> Presence is a delicious word ... nothing else can take the place of presence, not gifts, nor telephone calls, not pictures, not mementos, nothing ... When we are ill, we don't need soothing words nearly as much as we need loved ones to be present. What makes shared life – games, walks, concerts, outings and a myriad of other things – so pleasurable? Presence.[6]

We can be people who show up, turn up and stay put when life is tough for our friends and neighbours. Actions speak so much more loudly than words. Some of us are good at 999-type calls – we respond well to emergency situations. Others are better at serving the long-term needs of those around us – providing meals for the elderly or sick, helping out with the children of single-parent families, or being a support for someone in financial need. Each of us has a part to play to take the presence of Christ into the crises around us. Who are you present for at this time? Who needs your love and attention, and more than that, your time and presence?

PEOPLE OF TOUCH

Leo Buscaglia writes: 'Too often we underestimate the power of a touch, a smile, a kind word, a listening ear, an honest compliment, or the smallest act of caring, all of which have the potential to turn a life around.'[7]

Many years ago, an experiment at the maternity unit of the Bellevue Hospital in New York showed that the mortality rate for infants under one year old fell from 35 per cent to less than 10 per cent if the babies were picked up, carried around and 'mothered' several times a day. Similar findings have been noted in Eastern European orphanages. If the lack of touch is a contributory factor to physical death, what does lack of touch mean in terms of relationships?

Obviously we need to be aware that touch for some people is unwanted and concerning. Those who have been damaged by inappropriate relationships may not be able to show affection through touch or want it in return. But touch is certainly very powerful.

There was once a young mother, nervously waiting for her daughter's new playgroup to open. She didn't know anyone, as the council had only recently moved her to the village. The other mums all seemed to be chatting away and she felt left out, but too shy to join in the conversation. Another mum arrived with her child and sat next to the anxious parent. She patted her on the arm and smiled. 'Noisy here, isn't it?'

'Yeah!' the young mum agreed, smiling back.

'You'll get used to it. We may be noisy, but we are good at listening too.' The other mother stroked the little girl's hair and asked her name.

Weeks later, that single parent thanked the woman for reaching out to her and her daughter that day. It made such a difference to the way she felt about living in the area, and her child starting at the playgroup. More than that, it gave her the confidence to invite a few of the mums round for coffee and was the start of some meaningful relationships.

We cannot underestimate the power of physical touch.

Scripture gives us advice on how we can greet one another: 2 Corinthians 13:12, Romans 16:16 and several other verses say we should greet one another with a holy kiss! However, some churches are definitely handshaking churches, some are hugging churches, and a few are kissing churches. (I have heard that the difference between a normal kiss and a holy kiss is about two minutes!)

But seriously, we are not meant to be people who are reticent to show our feelings and be welcoming to others. We are meant to demonstrate love in how we treat one another in both our words and our actions.

PE⊕PLE WH⊕ LISTEN

It has been said that our inability to communicate is a result of our failure to listen effectively. I remember talking to someone who was in a difficult situation. They said, 'It's really easy to work out who the people are who really care.'

'How's that?' I responded.

'Mick, it's simple. It's those people who truly listen.'

Sometimes we are all too ready with a quick-fix answer when someone shares a need with us, aren't we? But often what people actually want is a sounding board – someone who will simply allow them to offload. In 2006 I was diagnosed with cancer. More often than not, as I shared this information with people, they felt as though it was it was their responsibility to say something deep, meaningful and of significance to me. So they would come up with a truth or a good statement, or they would give me advice or tell me about their dad's secretary's brother's cancer. Very few actually properly *listened*.

Good listening takes practice. The truth is that most of us are much better at talking than listening. But listening is vital if we are going to develop and invest in good, healthy relationships, because it involves being just as aware of the other person's needs as you are of your own.

I've failed in this many times myself. I come in from work and I see my wife, who asks, 'How was your day?' and I reply, 'It's been OK. What about you?' And she says, 'I've had a terrible sore throat today ...' and I immediately respond with, 'Yeah, me too!' What I've done is to immediately bring the conversation back round to me. I have 'sort of' listened to her, but instinctively I am talking about myself again. If I took a group picture of your church family and put it on my Facebook page, who would you look for first? Yes, yourself! We instinctively look at things from a point of view of self-interest. We need to learn not to be so focused on ourselves. Paul gave us some very straightforward and valuable advice on this front:

> Do nothing out of selfish ambition or vain conceit, but in humility consider others better than yourselves. Each of you should look not only to your own interests, but also to the interests of others. Your attitude should be the same as that of Christ Jesus: Who, being in very nature God, did not consider equality with God something to be grasped ...
>
> Phil. 2:3–6

Or, as *The Message* puts verse 4:

> Put yourself aside, and help others get ahead. Don't be obsessed with getting your own advantage. Forget yourselves long enough to lend a helping hand.

GOD IS A LISTENING GOD

I am so thankful that when I come before God He doesn't interrupt me and say, 'Well, I know all about that, Mick! I'm omniscient, remember? Don't bother me with this. I've heard it all before.' Can you imagine how that would feel?

I'm so glad He's not like that. He lets me come into His presence and talk and pray and He never shouts me down! When Jesus walked alongside those two disciples on the road to Emmaus, He could have simply silenced them and said, 'Look, can I stop you there? I am Jesus! So, shall we cut to the chase? I'm a busy man!' Why didn't He do that? Because He was prepared to wait and allow them to express their hearts to Him. He encouraged them, He let them talk and share their concerns. Then He revealed who He was, *after* He had listened. We would do well to follow this same principle in our own lives. Proverbs 18:13 says, 'He who answers before listening – that is his folly and his shame'. Isn't that challenging?

Good listening involves not thinking about what you are going to say while the other person is still talking. Figuring out what *you* are going to say before they have finished means you've not really heard what they've said in the first place!

I'm a bit of a people watcher. I'm happy to sit in a café and watch the world go by. Sometimes when I've overheard people chatting, I've discovered that they are just taking it in turns to talk but are not actually involved in a proper conversation. There is no real 'listening' going on! I had to learn this when I was involved in small group psychotherapy. I was always terrible at jumping in too quickly because I wasn't comfortable with silence, so my supervisors would make me count to a certain number in my head causing me to wait. (You might think that is really extreme, but I had to start somewhere!) Silence can sometimes feel longer than it really is, but it is very helpful if you are evaluating what someone is saying.

Good relationships involve non-judgmental listening. Maybe reflecting back what a person has said is valuable, because often we don't get it right. Sometimes we think we've heard someone say something, but actually when we repeat it back to them, they've not said that at all. Often when people are talking to us, they use words to skirt around the edges of something deeper they would like to communicate. Very often, when people are having problems in life, their words are littered with clues as to the deeper roots of their issues. Learning to be a good listener can help you to read in between the lines of people's words, rather than taking them at face value. Henry Nouwen said that, 'Listening is the highest form of hospitality'. To really listen to someone also pays them a great honour. It shows respect and deference.

How good are you at listening? One of the selection criteria for finding counsellors for a teenage camp was this exercise. The applicants were given the following simple statement:

> A young person comes to you and says, 'I'm tired of pleasing my parents and nothing I do seems to be right and I'm just about to give up.'
> How would you respond to that?

Of the 3,001 applicants, 2,893 missed the point. Most of the people responded with 'fix it' type statements like, 'I'm sure your parents mean well … ' or 'Maybe you need to spend more time with them …' The people who were ultimately hired as counsellors were the ones who responded with empathetic 'listening' type responses such as, 'It sounds like you are having a really difficult time'.

Those who really listened acknowledged the problem without trying to solve it. Sometimes as parents, we're quick to talk and slow to listen. We carried out a similar exercise on one of our counselling courses at CWR and a woman came back the next week and said it had revolutionised her family life. She said, 'My daughter came in from school the other day and she threw her bags down in the hallway

saying, "I hate school! I'm never going to go back there again."'
Previously this mother would have said, 'Well, yes you are! Pick this
stuff up. Don't be ridiculous, saying you are not going back to school.
What on earth are you talking about?' But instead, the mother just
said, 'It sounds like you've had a bad day.' Her daughter said, 'It's been
terrible, Mum … ' And they sat down and talked things through
without having the usual 'confrontation' they were used to.

Are you too quick to tell people what you think they need to do
or hear? Do you need to just acknowledge, with them, that you have
'heard' their issues?

KNOWN FOR OUR LOVE

What are we known for as Christians?

In 2007, authors David Kinnaman and Gabe Lyons published a
book called *UnChristian*[8] which brought together the findings of
extensive research among 16- to 29-year-olds of their perception
of Christians. It makes for quite chilling reading, and the authors
contend that Christians have taken some giant steps backwards in
their most essential earthly assignment. One of the top answers given
in response to the question, 'What do you think of when you hear the
word "Christian"?' was 'Anti-Gay'. Nothing to do with the Church,
God or acts of kindness sprang to mind, but rather right-wing politics
and negative, critical, judgmental attitudes.

Often in dealing with people who have little understanding of the
Christian faith our default starting point has to be to undo a great
many preconceptions that are really unhelpful. Why is it that people
can misunderstand what we Christians are about so easily?

Partly it is because we have not been good at modelling our faith.
We are not always seen to speak the truth with love. We are not
always perfect in our relationships. I heard a story about a husband

and his wife who were on a camping trip in bad weather. They were not enjoying it all. In the morning, after their tent had leaked badly, the wife asked her husband, 'Do I look like a water buffalo?' He looked at her and responded, 'If I tell you the truth, do you promise not to charge?' There is a way of handling truth and it is always with love and encouragement!

Hebrews 3:13 speaks about the need daily to encourage one another. I find that really challenging. Sometimes we're too discouraged ourselves to encourage anyone else. But the result of encouragement is always to make people thrive.

John 13:34–35 says:

> 'A new command I give you: Love one another. As I have loved you, so you must love one another. By this all men will know that you are my disciples, if you love one another.'

God wants us to be experts in the art of living. In the Church we've been fantastic obstetricians, but not very good paediatricians. We can bring people into the Church, but we are not always good at caring for them when they are there.

KNOWN FOR CARING

In times of trouble and distress, people aren't interested in what we know. People often don't care about our theology or what we believe when life throws them a curve ball. They're not interested in what our particular take on eschatology is or the deep intricacies of doctrine or theology, they just want to know that we care about them. I've never met anyone, for example, who, when struggling with the difficulties of a harsh marriage or a stillborn child or a life-threatening illness has wanted to enter into major doctrinal debate.

They just want to know, where is Jesus and does He care? They ask questions like, 'Do I matter?' 'Am I important to God?' People aren't interested in what we know; they want to know that we care.

Our role as God's ambassadors on earth is to love others as Christ has loved us. There is no higher calling than to be relational in the way that He is.

life IN BETWEEN

'Every action of our lives
touches on some chord that
will vibrate in eternity.'

E.H. CHAPIN

05

Another aspect of our journey of faith, hope, love and everything in between that we need to consider is – how we live our lives in the light of eternity. Let me preface my comments by highlighting and emphasising that this chapter is not intended to be an in-depth theological examination or exegesis of heaven. Neither is it an apologetic for a particular 'end time' viewpoint. What it is, I hope, is an honest exploration of the disquiet every one of us feels in our souls regarding eternity – that unnamed, slightly intangible restlessness that we each need to come to terms with if we are to truly mature in our walk with God.

Jerome P. Crabb once quipped, 'Dying is like getting audited by the IRS – something that only happens to other people … until it happens to you.' This illustrates the way in which many people think about life or, more specifically, death. In other words, they try *not* to think about it at all, preferring to take a 'head in the sand' approach. As Woody Allen once said, 'It's not that I'm afraid to die, I just don't want to be there when it happens!'[1]

As followers of Jesus we shouldn't need to make death the taboo topic that others do, because we know we have eternal hope in Christ. Yet, the truth is, many Christians find it just as difficult to come to terms with their own mortality. We employ sophisticated, subtle strategies to distract ourselves from thinking about the day when we will have to face the inevitable. But inevitable it is. As someone else has said, 'The mortality rate is still running at 100 per cent. None of us get out of here alive!'

I vividly remember a number of occasions when Selwyn Hughes

ministered during the later stages of his cancer. It had spread to his bones and this made standing, even for short periods of time, extremely painful, so he would speak sitting down. He would sometimes begin his talk by saying, 'I'm dying, you know.' This frequently stunned or at least unsettled his listeners and he would try to reassure them that it probably wouldn't happen during his talk! But he did it to underline the fact that death is inevitable for us all, and to stress why it is so important to consider how we live our lives *now*. We need to live with a clear view of eternity.

In my experience, anyone who has had a close shave with death will change their outlook and approach to life – often radically. Those who have escaped the clutches of a life-threatening illness, for instance, will generally re-enter life with renewed energy and enthusiasm. Such experiences tend to change people's minds about issues of faith and belief.

The truth is, once we have glimpsed eternity, it totally changes our perspective. It affects our motivation, the choices we make on a daily basis, how we nurture our relationships, and so many other aspects of life.

Someone once said that 'a journey is only as good as its ending'. The more I think about this statement, the more profound it becomes. Isn't this what most people fear – that life itself is meaningless, leading to nothing, and that when we die, that's it – game over? Or perhaps that we might have lived our life without ever really fulfilling our true potential?

Without the prospect of an exciting and certain destination at the end of our journey to draw us on in eager anticipation, then yes, life should be viewed as tragic indeed – a nightmare of endless restlessness and uncomfortable struggling. The existential philosopher, John-Paul Sartre, said, 'Life has no meaning the moment you lose the illusion of being eternal.' Sartre didn't believe in the existence of a Creator, but even he could see that without some understanding of 'eternity', life is futile. Followers of many of the newer spiritualities and older world religions try to work around this problem of futility by suggesting that life is a never-ending cycle of birth and death – that we die and are then reborn, and we try to live a better life the next time around. Personally I don't find this a very cheery prospect. If that is all I had to believe in, then life could become very miserable. The apostle Paul felt the same: 'If the dead are not raised', he says in 1 Corinthians 15:32, '"Let us eat and drink, for tomorrow we die"'. In other words, if this life, here and now, is as good as it gets, then we may as well get drunk or eat as much cake as we like, and live however we see fit.

Personally, I don't believe that 'here and now' is all there is. The Bible teaches us that we have an eternity with God to look forward to. But we can easily lose sight of that truth in the malaise and hard work of daily living.

LOSING SIGHT OF HOPE

One of the key reasons, I believe, why Christians struggle with the issue of their mortality is that they have forgotten the hope to which they have been called. Gabriel Marcel said that 'Hope is for the soul what breathing is for the living organism'. Paul writes in 1 Corinthians 13:13:

> And now these three remain: faith, *hope* and love. But the greatest of these is love. (Italics mine)

Love may be the greatest quality we can possess, but both love and faith depend upon *hope*. Hope plays the decisive role. Later in Colossians 1:5 we read about 'the faith and love that spring from the *hope* that is stored up for you in heaven'.

Our courage for the spiritual journey so often falters because we lose sight of our hope for heaven – our eternal destination, the consummation of our journey. We get so wrapped up in our earthly existence that we forget we are citizens of another kingdom. In his book *The Eclipse of Heaven*, A.J. Conyers sums it up succinctly when he writes:

> We live in a world no longer under heaven ... much of the rage and deadness that simmers just beneath the surface of our Christian façade has a common root – we live in this world and have no expectation of the world to come.[2]

Most of the emotional problems we struggle with, Conyers claims, stem from this blinkeredness regarding eternity. Take away the hope of arrival at the end of our journey and our journey becomes meaningless, empty, and devoid of pleasure.

ETERNITY IN OUR HEARTS

It's impossible to ignore our mortality – we all have to face up to it. We are born, we grow and mature, we age continually, and eventually our bodies wear out and cease functioning. Trying to suspend or reverse this process is ultimately a futile exercise, and because it's a mission doomed to failure, trying will just serve to increase the sense of restlessness and discomfort we feel, leading to more emotional turbulence, and ultimately to anxiety and fear. One only has to consider the statistics regarding cosmetic surgery to see how immensely determined people have become to retain at least the appearance of their youth, with the number of procedures performed rising steadily year on year, and the nature of the procedures themselves becoming more outlandish.

WHY DOES ALL OF THIS GO AGAINST THE GRAIN?

Firstly, the Bible speaks at length about the honour that accompanies the wisdom which only comes through age and maturity. But secondly, and more fundamentally, God has placed inside us a kind of 'homing beacon' designed to lead us ever closer to heaven, our destination. The writer of Ecclesiastes puts it in these words: 'He has also set eternity in the hearts of men ...' (Eccl. 3:11). This suggests that when God designed us, He deliberately and purposefully placed in us a longing for eternity. The world has subverted this longing and turned it into a desire to stretch out our existence in this physical realm for as long as possible, but God's intention is for us to experience eternity with Him.

Wordsworth captured this truth in his poem 'Intimations of Immortality'. He expresses it like this:

> Our birth is but a sleep and a forgetting,
> The soul that rises with us, our life's star,
> Hath elsewhere its setting,
> And cometh from afar:
> Not in entire forgetfulness,
> And not in utter nakedness,
> But trailing clouds of glory do we come
> From God who is our home.

The line that is most striking for me is 'From God who is our home'. The fact that we came from God accounts for the mysterious homesickness we feel – that sense of 'something is not quite right' which occupies every human heart. We were made by God for God, and that restlessness will never go away until we return and find our home in God.

The journalist and author Malcolm Muggeridge, in his book *Jesus*

Rediscovered, recalled how, since he was a boy, he had had the sense of being a stranger in this world, and was certain there was a world beyond this to which he felt he was moving. He wrote:

> I strain my ears to hear the distant music, my eyes to see the bright light far away. The only ultimate disaster that can befall us, I have come to realise, is to feel ourselves to be at home here on earth. As long as we are aliens we cannot forget our true homeland.[3]

SPIRITUAL HOMESICKNESS

The good news of the gospel message makes the source of this longing for eternity, this hunger of the soul, apparent to us. But most men and women in the world don't quite know what is wrong with them. They are aware of feelings of being a small part of 'something bigger' than themselves at times, and they reach out in various ways in the hope that 'the stars' or some kind of supernatural force will speak to them about their destiny. But although they know they are longing for something, they can't clearly describe it. They can't quite place their finger on the issue or name it properly.

We could accurately describe these 'homesick' feelings of longing for 'something' as a kind of *nostalgia*. The word 'nostalgia' comes from two Greek words – *nostos*, meaning 'to return home', and *algos* meaning 'pain' – literally, an anguish to return home. As one Christian psychiatrist said, 'Homesickness is the one common malady of mankind out of which all other problems emerge.'

WHAT DID HE MEAN?

Simply that 'homesickness' can only be cured by one thing: *home*. Our human hearts yearn for God, our home. That is why all the other strategies people employ to satisfy this yearning are doomed to failure. Money, fame and pleasure don't relieve the homesickness. Potentially satisfying relationships with our family, our friends or our spouses can't totally obliterate it, either.

We simply can't deny or ignore this longing which God Himself has placed within us. If we do, it results in deadening that part of our soul that aches for Him – and this deadness results in such a level of discomfort in our personality that it can only be assuaged by yet more denial or more attempts to satisfy the ache in ways that don't lead to God. We find ourselves trapped in a vicious circle which ultimately places us in peril. No sense of true security or significance exists where God is not present – and without security and significance we are easy prey for a multitude of emotional problems. C.S. Lewis said that if we find in ourselves desires which this world cannot satisfy, then the only logical explanation is that we were made for another world.[4] And Paul, writing about eternity, says in 1 Corinthians 15:19, 'If only for this life we have hope in Christ, we are to be pitied more than all men'.

Perhaps we don't think enough about the end of our journey because of our embedded world-view and preconceived ideas? Let's face it, some of the images people have of heaven as John Eldredge says[5] are strange – fat babies fluttering around with tiny wings, or bored saints lazing on shapeless clouds, strumming harps and wondering what's happening back on earth – and unbiblical to say the least!

The Catholic philosopher Peter Kreeft expressed it this way, saying that the crisis of hope that afflicts the Church today is a crisis of imagination:

> Our pictures of heaven are dull, platitudinous and syrupy, therefore so is our faith our hope and love of heaven. Dullness, not doubt, is the strongest enemy of our faith, just as indifference not hate is the strongest enemy of love.[6]

If this is true, and I believe it is, shouldn't we devote ourselves to recovering a vision for the end of our journey in as vivid colours as our imaginations can conceive?

The reality of heaven is so amazingly different! Paul writes:

> ... no mind has conceived what God has prepared for those who love him.
>
> 1 Cor. 2:9

And the brief glimpses that we see of eternity when for an instant the curtain between this side of time and that is lifted, reveal an adventure of intimacy, beauty and joy. Heaven will be the fulfilment of all our longings where we are fully embraced into God's other-centred relationship with us.

TOO HEAVENLY MINDED?

Having made the argument for us being much more conscious of the eternal aspect of our lives, I realise that it invites the criticism that some Christians are so heavenly minded as to be of no earthly use. Caricatures spring to mind of saintly people constantly engaged in prayer, oblivious to the needs of the world around them. But this is unfair. My reading of history tells me that the great and the godly of the past managed to live their lives firmly rooted on earth, addressing the needs of those around them, whilst always keeping heaven in view. Does the prospect of heaven before us make us less keen to serve those around us on earth? If so, then there is something seriously wrong! Often the Christians who accomplished the most for our world were those who thought a good deal about the next. Some of society's greatest social reformers – John Wesley, Lord Shaftesbury, William Booth, George Muller – were men who kept heaven in view, and because of that were motivated by a godly desire to accomplish as much as possible this side of eternity. With energy, skill and determination they endeavoured to bring about the outworking of God's purposes on earth, yet they had complete confidence in heaven as their final destination, and talked about it often.

If the truth be told, most of us go through life with our eyes focused downwards – we neither look for nor long for heaven. In which case, we should not be surprised if we find that earthly concerns become more important to us than heavenly ones. Unless we take time to regularly gaze into eternity, then *time* becomes more important than *eternity*. But men such as Wesley, Shaftesbury and Booth understood that 'Every action of our lives touches on some chord that will vibrate in eternity', as the playwright Sean O'Casey wrote. Their ministry was effective on earth because they saw God's bigger picture. They journeyed on earth with our heavenly destination in mind. I believe we will work better for God here on earth when, by faith, we keep the perfect end in view. When we are consumed by looking forward to what lies ahead, it provides us with a constant reminder that no matter how permanent the things that make up our life may seem, they are in fact fleeting and temporal.

DIVERSIONS

Thomas Watson expressed a similar thought when he wrote: 'The world is but a great inn, where we are to stay a night or two and be gone; what madness is it so to set our heart upon our inn, as to forget our home.' The singer-songwriter Larry Norman expressed the same thing very simply and profoundly when he said that he was just passing through, for this world was not his home.[7] Both writers had the same thought in mind: the material things for which so many crave become less and less important in the eyes of those who are drawing ever closer to God. They see them as no more important than the furnishings of an inn they might stay at for just one night. Heaven, on the other hand, is our *home*. It's where we *belong*. We are bound for a 'city ... whose architect and builder is God' (Heb. 11:10). When we keep this truth in view, we can learn to hold onto things more lightly, understanding that they are temporal.

One of the biggest deceptions a person can fall into is to be robbed of the awareness of our 'home' – God our home, and eternity our final destination. Our enemy therefore goes to great lengths to try to ensure that men and women don't interpret the yearnings they feel inside as yearning for God. He has two main tactics: one is to encourage us to escape such feelings by going on long detours that really lead nowhere – to experiment and try all manner of alternatives to quench the hunger of our soul. The second tactic is to convince us to reduce these yearnings to manageable proportions.

In C.S. Lewis's *The Silver Chair*,[8] there is a section in which the beautiful Queen of the Underworld tries to convince the children from the Overworld that her dismal kingdom is the only reality and that their world is but an imagined dream. She tries to convince them that there is no sun, and that they have only imagined it because they have seen her lamps. This is the mental strategy adopted by so many to 'explain away' our internal longing for the transcendent and eternal – especially those who subscribe to the so called 'psychological society'. I heard one psychologist claim on television recently that sexuality explains the yearnings we all have – and that when Christians say we are yearning for heaven, it is just a desire to return to the womb.

People will look to all kinds of solutions – whatever appeals to them – to appease the spiritual emptiness they feel. They recognise they are in emotional pain, so they look to make themselves and their surroundings as comfortable as possible – to try to find or create heaven on earth. It is reminiscent of the fallen angels in Milton's

Paradise Lost[9] who, upon reaching the black, burning pit, tried to convince one another that it wasn't really such a bad place! So many people spend their lives trying to convince themselves and those around them that despite the ugliness in the world, it is actually a beautiful place and we can and should all live happily ever after. Unfortunately, such a perspective ignores the disease of sin that exists in every human heart which humankind is powerless to eradicate. William Kirkpatrick made this point:

> The healthy mind works upwards, not downwards. It sees a sun-lamp and thinks of the sun – not the other way around.

Sin desensitises the soul to such a degree that many people hardly stop to acknowledge their yearning for eternity. They accept the lower rather than reaching for the higher. They settle for a sun-lamp instead of the sun.

Those who live without a vision of heaven discover, like Alice in Wonderland, that they are growing ever smaller, and their world is growing smaller along with them. They fail to grasp how expansive and exciting their world could be, viewed from the perspective of eternity. A world such as this, beautiful or comfortable as it may be, is not good enough to be called 'home'. A waiting room, yes; temporary accommodation, definitely. But not 'home'.

THE NOW AND THE NOT YET

We live in between two perfect places – the garden of God in Eden and the city of God in the time to come. The garden in which we are presently living is one that has been cursed, and although it is still quite beautiful in many places, it has an abundant supply of thorns and weeds. We were designed for a world much different in nature to the one we are currently occupying. The Garden of Eden was perfection; no struggling with sickness, wrestling with guilt or undergoing bouts of depression and misery. Because of what Christ accomplished for us on the cross we can know forgiveness for our sins, a cure for the yearnings deep within, and the promise of the Holy Spirit's help as we continue our journey and make our way through this world.

But for all that, it is still a world in measure for which we were not originally designed. This is why even when we experience joy in this life it is still in measure 'marred' joy. By that I mean that even in our happiest moments we experience a niggling sadness that arises from the fact that we are in an unnatural environment and nothing will ever feel quite right until we are home. In our very best moments we are aware that what we are experiencing, as good as it may be, is not the fullness of what we were made for. This is not negative thinking, it is realism. And facing the reality does not diminish the joy; rather it helps prevent us from pretending that what we have is better than it is. This is Christian realism – a factor missing in some sections of today's Church.

Someone has described this as the tension of living in 'the now and the not yet'. When we accept Christ as our Lord and Saviour, in a very real sense heaven is brought to earth – yet the world remains flawed and imperfect. We have to come to terms with this 'tension', otherwise we will become disillusioned and disappointed. Oswald Chambers was right when he said, 'Life is more tragic than orderly'. This is a tough world – a world still reeling from the effects of the Fall. Not to recognise or understand this may mean our expectations will be higher than they should be and our disappointments deeper than they need be. The Church needs a theology of suffering to balance its theology of miracles.

Reading the apostle Paul's discourse in 2 Corinthians 4:5–18 it is evident that he experienced the same difficulties as we do, grappling with the tension of the 'now and not yet'. But he managed to keep his eyes fixed on the unseen goal ahead of him:

> We are hard pressed on every side, but not crushed; perplexed, but not in despair; persecuted, but not abandoned; struck down, but not destroyed ... Therefore we do not lose heart. Though outwardly we are wasting away, yet inwardly we are being renewed day by day. For our light and momentary troubles are achieving for us an eternal glory that far outweighs them all. So we fix our eyes not on what is seen, but on what is unseen. For what is seen is temporary, but what is unseen is eternal.
>
> 2 Cor. 4:8–18

Paul was struggling, but he was struggling well. Though he was, at times, utterly perplexed by the world around him, he never shifted his focus away from heaven. He knew that there was a better world to come, and the prospect of it helped him to move forward. It always does. Critics of Christianity call this misguided escapism, but one could never call Paul an escapist – several times he was almost beaten to death for his faith. He faced the reality of heaven so that he could better face the realities of earth. Living with such a tension is not easy, but it is possible. Paul lived it and so can we.

HOPE

Throughout the Church's history, God's people have drawn comfort, when faced by life's struggles and problems, from the promise of heaven. The promise that one day we will be with Jesus in a perfect world can have a powerful effect on our lives in this present realm and enable us to cope with difficult situations, because it gives us that most precious of all ingredients: *hope*. Proverbs 13:12 says:

> Hope deferred makes the heart sick, but a longing fulfilled is a tree of life.

Hope in our heavenly destination gives us a correct perspective on life. One speaker I heard a while ago remarked that the apostle Paul was always eager to go to heaven, but willing to stay on earth. 'We are willing to go,' he said, 'but eager to stay.' Notice how often in the Scriptures Paul uses the prospect of heaven to help him overcome the trials of life. 'I consider that our present sufferings are not worth comparing with the glory that will be revealed in us', he writes in Romans 8:18. I once heard someone say, 'Here on earth there is something wrong with everything. In heaven there will be nothing wrong with anything.' Such hope gives us tremendous reassurance and comfort.

A colleague of mine, when I was working in a large hospital, once commented to me that she had noticed Christians handled death in a much better way than those who weren't believers. I asked her why she thought this was the case. After pausing for a few moments she replied, 'I suppose it's because Christians have a hope beyond the grave.' Simple, but profound. We have 'hope'. But what is hope? People have defined it in various ways. For some, hope is a fragile commodity, a precarious thing that might easily be snatched away. This is not the quality of hope described in the New Testament. Biblical hope is rock solid, and Paul teaches that it is one of the defining, cardinal virtues of the Christian life. Those who view hope as elusive and fragile are not talking about the same kind of hope! There is real (biblical) hope, and then there is counterfeit hope.

There is a story about the painting by G.F. Watts entitled *Hope*. The picture shows a blindfolded woman sitting with bowed head on a sphere, holding a lyre in her hand. All the strings of the lyre are broken except one, and only one star shines in the darkened sky and it's true to say that those who do not understand symbols find the meaning difficult to grasp. The story goes that two street people, who had crept into the gallery to escape from the cold, looked up at the painting. One commented, '*Hope*? Why is it called *Hope*?' The other, gazing at the figure perched precariously on the sphere, replied, 'I suppose because she hopes she won't fall off.'

Hope is not 'hoping we won't fall off'. What the world describes as hope is often nothing more than optimism. Optimism has to be a better option than pessimism, of course, but it is no replacement for *real hope*. The hope of Christians is the hope of eternal life in which death is not the end but merely a door, a point of entry into eternity with Christ. Our hope is founded on the death and resurrection of Jesus, who not only proclaimed life after death, but demonstrated it. Without that demonstration, hope is just words. But with it, hope has everything going for it.

CITIZENS OF HEAVEN

We have seen that we are to live on earth as more than just tourists visiting from another country whilst acknowledging that ultimately heaven is our home. The hope of our home in heaven is sure and certain. Even though we were born on earth, when we come to know Christ it is as if God issues us with new passports. We are here temporarily, we don't belong here. In Hauerwas and Willimon's book *Resident Aliens*, they say: 'The Jews in Dispersion were well acquainted with what it meant to live as strangers in a strange land, aliens trying to stake out a living in someone's else's turf.[10]

Anyone wanting to become a naturalised US citizen has to renounce any prior citizenship during the 'naturalisation ceremony'. In a similar way, once we commit ourselves to Christ, we are giving up our earthly citizenship to become citizens of heaven. Paul uses this phrase in Philippians 3:20–21:

> But our citizenship is in heaven. And we eagerly await a Saviour from there, the Lord Jesus Christ, who, by the power that enables him to bring everything under his control, will transform our lowly bodies so that they will be like his glorious body.

What does being a 'citizen of heaven' involve? Let's take a close look at the context of these verses.

Paul has just been talking about some antagonists of the gospel message, whom he describes as having their minds 'set on earthly things' (Phil. 3:19). True Christians, he says, look towards the eternal and have their minds set on what is above. Philippi had the distinction of being a Roman colony, with all the privileges that brought with it in the ancient world, but Paul wanted his Philippian readers to understand that they had a higher allegiance than Rome – they were citizens of heaven.

To be a citizen of heaven means that though during our life here on earth we obey the laws of the state, pay our taxes and act honourably and honestly in every circumstance, our supreme loyalty and love lie elsewhere. It is heaven's government that ultimately guides and directs our lives, and it is the mind of the King in heaven that we seek to know most of all.

Hauerwas and Willimon go on to say:

> A colony is a beachhead, an outpost, an island of one culture
> in the middle of another; a place where the values of home
> are reiterated and passed on to the young; a place where the
> distinctive language and lifestyle of the resident aliens are
> lovingly nurtured and reinforced.[11]

This 'alien world' we live in influences us all. Its judgments affect us, its atmosphere is not conducive to our spiritual development and its pressures bear down on us in innumerable ways. It is easy for us, without realising it, to be conformed to this world. Paul warns us against this in Romans 12:2. Instead, we aim to live as loyal subjects of the country we call home. We are citizens of heaven. More than that, we are ambassadors of our heavenly country.

> We are therefore Christ's ambassadors, as though God were
> making his appeal through us.
>
> 2 Cor. 5:20

An ambassador is a personal representative of his or her nation and its head of state. It is an immense honour and privilege to be called to be an ambassador of one's country. But, of course, such a role is not without its dangers. According to Samuel Hoare in his book *Ambassador on Special Mission,*

> one of the dangers an ambassador faces is staying too long
> in the country to which he has been sent; that is to say, if
> he does not make frequent visits to his own land, breathe
> his own native air, reacquaint himself with his native
> customs and familiarise himself with all that is going on,
> he can quickly become 'denationalised'. He must return
> home frequently, absorb his own atmosphere, renew his

strength by contact with his native soil, so that he does not lose his orientation.[12]

How can we, as citizens of heaven, save ourselves from being not so much 'denationalised' as 'despiritualised'? We do so by continually breathing the atmosphere of heaven by talking to God constantly through prayer, by meditating on His Word and by setting our 'hearts on things above, where Christ is seated at the right hand of God' (Col. 3:1).

A friend of mine was once told the following:

> One of the secrets of success in the Christian life is to realise that now you have a new nationality. You may be British (or from some other nation) by natural birth, but because you have been born again, you are now a citizen of heaven. If ever heaven's rule conflicts with earth's domain, then remember, heaven's rule must take precedence.

He added,

> And remember, too, that the secret of success in prayer is to guard your time with God. Speak to Him, listen to Him, and count as dangerous anything that causes you to lose your links with heaven.

Those words – 'count as dangerous anything that causes you to lose your links with heaven' – resonate with me. There is no way that a Christian ambassador can retain their true citizenship in this alien world without regular prayer and meditation on the Scriptures. We must return whenever we can to our own environment, maintain our Christian world-view – not be conformed to the world. And because we are, by nature, forgetful, we must revisit again and again the words of the writer of Hebrews:

> Let us fix our eyes on Jesus, the author and perfecter of
> our faith, who for the joy set before him endured the cross,
> scorning its shame, and sat down at the right hand of the
> throne of God. Consider him who endured such opposition
> from sinful men, so that you will not grow weary and
> lose heart.
>
> Heb. 12:2–3

One of the greatest challenges we all experience on our journey is
this tendency to forget – to forget where we are bound, to forget
God's past goodness to us, to forget our hope. This is why the Bible
is full of exhortations to remember! I love *The Message* translation of
the above verses:

> Keep your eyes on *Jesus*, who both began and finished this
> race we're in. Study how he did it. Because he never lost
> sight of where he was headed – that exhilarating finish
> in and with God – he could put up with anything along
> the way: Cross, shame, whatever. And now he's *there*, in
> the place of honour, right alongside God. When you find
> yourselves flagging in your faith, go over that story again,
> item by item, that long litany of hostility he ploughed
> through. That will shoot adrenaline into your souls!

All the while He was on earth, Jesus remembered where He was
headed. Without that heaven-centred internal compass we will find
this journey a struggle. Jesus never lost sight of where He was going
– He had a vision for the future that was grounded in the past. On
this journey of faith, hope, love and everything in between, He is

our model, our ultimate example.

But He is also the author and finisher of our faith. Though we may stumble through life at times, losing sight of our heavenly destination, He will neither forget nor desert us. We trust in Him, and this is why our hope is unshakeable.

life's BIG QUESTIONS

'To love means loving the
unlovable. To forgive means
pardoning the unpardonable.
Faith means believing the
unbelievable. Hope means
hoping when everything
seems hopeless.'

G.K. CHESTERTON[1]

06

THE CERTAINTY OF UNCERTAINTY

Jesus was very clear that we would experience difficulties on our journey of faith.

> 'I have told you these things, so that in me you may have peace. In this world you will have trouble. But take heart! I have overcome the world.'
>
> **John 16:33**

Notice that there are two definitive statements here:

1. We *will* have trouble.
2. He *has* overcome everything that the world can throw at us.

The Christian life is one where we have to handle a great deal of confusion, trouble and mystery. It's true to say that none of us are very good at this. We would all prefer it otherwise. It would be great if being a Christian meant that we were never afflicted by trouble and that all our questions were answered immediately. But sadly this is not the case!

John Lennon once remarked that life is what happens while we are making other plans. Everyone who walks along the path of faith will, sooner or later, meet with some confusion, mystery or fear. People have often asked me, 'Why can't God make His purposes clear to us, and relieve us from all the uncertainty and anxiety?' The truth is, the path we are called to share is often shrouded in mystery and filled with doubt of many kinds. Yet I believe we all need to learn to live with mystery. If there is one thing in life that *is* certain, it is that life is not at all certain – but that our God is wonderfully, powerfully and majestically 'an ever-present help in times of trouble'.

THE FUTILITY OF TRYING TO MANAGE MYSTERY

When we were looking at our world-view we acknowledged that there is a longing for heaven built into the human heart, and there are different ways in which most people deal with it. One way is to make a detour around it and try to avoid it altogether and go in another direction, busying ourselves with things that are less important. Another way is to face the fact that there *is* an inconsolable longing in the heart, but to reduce it to something classifiable and explainable. Dr Larry Crabb (previously known for his work in Christian counselling and now as a spiritual director) frequently expresses this point in his work. He says,

> Instead of sitting quietly before mystery, we try to bring it
> into the area of manageability. What fools we are.'[2]

We want to manage it. We want to understand it. When we do this, we shouldn't be surprised that the phenomenon of mystery gets a little bit out of shape. William Kirkpatrick, another psychologist, once said, 'It is like trying to fit size twelve shoes into a size four shoebox, or trying to stuff a bird of paradise into a canary cage. Once you cram it in there, it won't look like a bird of paradise anymore.'

This passion we have to explain the things we don't understand is our effort to bring them under our control. Yet, godly mystery is meant to be part and parcel of life. We are not meant to know, understand or be able to explain everything. To all who seek answers, Psalm 46:10 says, 'Be still, and know that I am God'.

The affairs of the soul often can't be 'managed'. Frequently, all we can do is bring them quietly into the presence of God, and trust Him.

I lived and worked overseas for a while. During a particularly difficult time, there was one point when my wife turned to me and said, 'Do you know what would really help? I need a ten-page letter from God explaining what's going on!' I know I have often felt the same, especially when I have been unsure of the next step. But sometimes God allows us to go through certain things in order for our trust in Him to deepen and grow.

Hope and loss, doubt and trust are key elements for us to get to grips with in life. Each of these is a component of 'mystery'. Why must we grapple with them? Because often it is when we are faced with a struggle that we really mature as followers of Christ. If we read Hebrews 11, the Bible's great 'hall of faith' passage, it is striking to notice that many of the men and women mentioned never lived to see the fruit of their prayers. They had to wait until they entered eternity to discover that God had honoured their faithfulness.

These heroes of faith had to live with mystery, but we are often impatient to understand the will of God. We ask questions such as:

> Why doesn't God speak to me?
> Why don't I know what to do in this situation?
> Why is God allowing this to happen?
> Why have I been made redundant?
> Why did my husband leave me?
> Why do I have this illness?

Sometimes we don't 'hear' any answer to such questions. Often our questions are met with silence – and the problem with silence is that we are tempted to try to fill in the gaps. We like action, so we start to panic and demand a response. We make up our own answers to the questions and try to second-guess God: 'It's because I'm not good enough ... I'm not worthy of His attention ... I don't pray enough, so no wonder God is ignoring me.' We manufacture such illusions as 'solutions' for ourselves.

LIVING WITH MYSTERY

We need to learn to live comfortably with confusion and mystery. But that's not easy, is it? I read an article in *The Guardian* recently where a columnist wrote that she liked the fact that the weather forecast was invariably wrong. 'It was a daily reminder', she said, 'of the ultimate ignorance of humankind – that there are huge things we cannot understand. I find this both healthy and humbling.'[3] We can watch the news with its up-to-the-minute developments regarding technology, and the scientific discoveries of our age are truly amazing. Yet there is *so much* we don't know. We just don't know that we don't know it!

I heard a story about a man who really liked 'Whodunnit'-type plays and thrillers. He decided to go and see a new production at his local theatre. Managing to get a seat for the opening night, he found he was sitting in a poor seat far from the stage. So he spoke to the usher: 'Listen, I've been waiting for this play to come to town for ages. Please can you get me a really good seat? I'm happy to pay you a good tip. I just want to be up at the front so I can see every nuance. I love solving mysteries like this, and I don't want to miss anything.' The usher nodded and found the man a great seat in the circle. He sat down and gave the usher a £1 coin. The usher looked at the coin, and then again at the man. 'Enjoy your evening, sir,' he said. 'Oh, and by the way, the butler did it in the parlour with the candlestick.'

The odd thing about mystery is that at one level we all enjoy it. We like a spot of intrigue and anticipation. So many movies, books and plays are based upon our desire to solve mysteries and puzzles. It's a paradox, but we love it and hate it at the same time. None of us really enjoys not knowing where we are going or what we are doing. But we quite like it in other people's lives. There is something majestic and noble about the mysterious, as long as it's not bothering me!

We live with such paradoxes all the time. We constantly hear oxymorons such as 'pretty ugly', 'peace force', 'friendly fire' or 'exact estimate'. We know what is meant by them, but we are forced to smile when we truly examine them. The Christian life is full of such paradoxes. The longer I live, the less I find I truly understand, and the more mystery I encounter. Children are a complete mystery to me. Microwaves are a mystery (I mean, exactly how do they work? I have no idea!). Mobile phones, DVDs and technology of many kinds – many of us don't actually know how they work, despite the fact that we use them day in and day out. But that tells me something. We don't have to know how it all works to be comfortable with it. We live comfortably side-by-side with it. We live side-by-side with mystery.

Take the Hadron Collider, for example. This is a tunnel that stretches for seventeen miles and is buried 600 feet underground. It took 10,000 scientists and engineers from 100 countries with a budget of £56 million to build it. Why did they do it? They are trying to understand the meaning of life. The whole purpose of this massive amount of collaborative technology is to try to find out how the universe began. If you read their website they say this:

> The Universe started with a Big Bang, but we don't fully
> understand how or why it developed that way. The Hadron
> Collider will let us see how matter behaved a tiny fraction

of a second after the Big Bang. Researchers have some ideas what to expect, but also expect the unexpected.[4]

Interestingly, the particle of matter these scientists are looking for has already been named 'The God Particle'. I find that amazing. In examining the astonishing world of micro particles, scientists are trying to understand the real miracle behind creation. Why? Because humanity is not comfortable with profound mystery. We want to feel better about our origins. We want to have an answer for things. Some people think that any answer is better than no answer.

THE REALITY OF MYSTERY

But the fact is there are many mysteries we will never solve. Søren Kierkegaard, the Danish philosopher and theologian, said, 'Life is not a problem to be solved, but a reality to be experienced.' We must resist the temptation to insist we understand everything we experience. As Psalm 139:6 says, 'Such knowledge is too wonderful for me, too lofty for me to attain'.

Writing about euthanasia in *Newsweek* in March 1997, Dr M. Scott Peck wrote that the loss of control plus the mystery, insecurity and irrationality of dying were also inherent to living.[5] In other words, we live in a mysterious world where all sorts of things happen that we will not understand.

Although we shouldn't be surprised, as God's revealed Word says:

'For my thoughts are not your thoughts, neither are your ways my ways,' declares the LORD. 'As the heavens are higher than the earth, so are my ways higher than your ways and my thoughts than your thoughts.'

Isa. 55:8–9

What a releasing truth this contains! We are not *meant* to know everything. Breathe a sigh of relief! Part of the order of the universe is that God's thought patterns and ways of doing things are higher than ours. They are purposefully out of reach to us. And yet, we have His wonderful promise later in verses 10–11 that everything He desires will be accomplished:

> 'As the rain and the snow come down from heaven, and do not return to it without watering the earth and making it bud and flourish, so that it yields seed for the sower and bread for the eater, so is my word that goes out from my mouth: It will not return to me empty, but will accomplish what I desire and achieve the purpose for which I sent it.'

What an amazing God!

THE MYSTERY OF HEAVEN

The story goes that Albert Einstein once boarded a train to Boston. He immediately began fumbling in his pocket for his ticket. The train's conductor noticed Einstein's frantic search as he checked the other passengers' tickets in the carriage. On arriving at Einstein's seat, the conductor asked the renowned scientist if he had a valid ticket. Einstein replied that he seemed to have misplaced it and had been searching for it. The conductor said, 'Mr Einstein, I, and everyone else on this train, know who you are and are sure you have a ticket. Rest assured that you have a seat on this train.' Einstein looked very relieved, but still puzzled as to his ticket's whereabouts. When the conductor finished checking the whole carriage, he walked down the aisle and noticed the scientist still looking for the lost ticket. 'Sir,' he said. 'I have total faith and confidence that you have a ticket. Please take your seat and be sure you can ride on this train.' At this Einstein replied, 'Thank you again, but I need to locate that train ticket to find out exactly where I am going!'

It is said that Billy Graham once told this story at an occasion to mark his ninetieth birthday. He then said, 'My children and grandchildren are telling me that I've gotten a little slovenly in my old age. I used to be a bit more fastidious. So I went out and bought a new suit for this luncheon and for one more occasion.' Graham looked intently at those gathered. 'You see before you the suit in which I'll be buried. But when you hear I'm dead, I don't want you to immediately remember the suit I'm wearing. I want you to remember this. I not only know who I am, I also know where I'm going.'[6]

How about you? How do you feel about the mystery of heaven? Do you feel certain of your eternal destiny, or do questions like that keep you awake in the middle of the night?

Despite the great many mysteries that life holds, the Bible is full of assurances and statements of faith that we can hang on to. Colossians 1:9–12 contains such a set of wonderful truths:

> For this reason, since the day we heard about you, we have not stopped praying for you and asking God to fill you with the knowledge of his will through all spiritual wisdom and understanding. And we pray this in order that you may live a life worthy of the Lord and may please him in every way: bearing fruit in every good work, growing in the knowledge of God, being strengthened with all power according to his glorious might so that you may have great endurance and patience, and joyfully giving thanks to the Father, who has qualified you to share in the inheritance of the saints in the kingdom of light.

THE MYSTERY OF SUFFERING

So we have said that life is not a problem to be solved, but a mystery to be lived. But it is not easy to live in that constant position of trust, especially when circumstances arise that make it seem God is not present or active in our lives, or when we are faced with crisis, doubt or illness.

Perhaps one of the greatest evidences of our ability to trust is our willingness to walk in the darkness when answers seem to elude us. An old Scandinavian proverb says, 'Faith is a bird that feels dawn breaking and sings while it is still dark.' Faith says that answers are not essential to living. We may *think* they are. But in reality we can cope with anything that is thrown at us when we have faith that God is with us. Secure in the knowledge of God's unwavering love and commitment to us, we can get through any situation.

Isaiah 43:1–5 assures us of this:

'Fear not, for I have redeemed you;
   I have summoned you by name; you are mine.
When you pass through the waters,
   I will be with you;
and when you pass through the rivers,
   they will not sweep over you.
When you walk through the fire,
   you will not be burned;
   the flames will not set you ablaze.
For I am the LORD, your God,
   the Holy One of Israel, your Saviour;
I give Egypt for your ransom,
   Cush and Seba in your stead.
Since you are precious and honoured in my sight,
   and because I love you,
I will give men in exchange for you,

and people in exchange for your life.
Do not be afraid, for I am with you …'

Notice that God says *when* we pass through the rivers, not *if*. Inevitably we will find ourselves in deep water, but God is very clear that we need not be afraid. We are 'precious and honoured' in His sight, and He will not abandon us.

We all need good, godly advice to help us get through life with all of its struggles, joys, ups and downs. Poor old Job in the Bible went through all sorts of incredibly difficult things, and longed for a bit of helpful advice. But his so-called friends, not to mention his wife, were far from useful to him. For verse after verse, we see Job suffering real difficulties. He lost his family and all his possessions. Everything was taken away from him. And his friends only add to his problems. Sometimes life can feel like this. It can seem as though we have been stripped of everything and everyone we have relied on. But the presence of God is a constant factor in our lives, and so we can trust His faithfulness.

One of my favourite worship songs, based on verses in Job, expresses this truth aptly – Matt Redman's 'Blessed be Your Name'. I love the lyrics, about blessing the name of the Lord through suffering, but they scare me too. Blessing the name of the Lord through the good times is one thing but the words go on to say blessed be His name in the tough times – singing this song always sobers me up a little.

However, at the end of all Job's difficulties, we see that he comes to a place of glorious surrender to God and is able to say:

'Though he slay me, yet will I hope in him. I will surely defend my ways to his face.'

Job 13:15

That's quite a declaration. Job had come to a place of deep reliance upon God. It is a place that we can come to as well. And in the midst of misery and confusion we can say, 'I don't see any sense in this, but I know that God, the Architect of this universe, has my life in His hands.'

THE MYSTERY OF DISASTER

Many people struggle with the question of how God can allow disasters to occur, or suffering to be part of the experience of so many of us. After all, isn't a loving God meant to alleviate and protect His children from pain? In seeking to look at this question, philosopher David Hume (echoing Epicurus) wrote ominously in 1776:

> Is God willing to prevent evil, but not able? Then he is impotent. Is he able, but not willing? Then he is malevolent.

The Christian world-view would incorporate the truth found in Ephesians 3:20,

> Now to him who is able to do immeasurably more than all we ask or imagine, according to his power that is at work within us ...

But that still leaves the question, 'If He is able, why then does He not always intervene?' Ultimately, of course, we do not know. But we trust in a God who is good – that is the essence of faith.

It is said that Charles Darwin did not lose his faith in God because of the theory of evolution he developed, but because of his personal sufferings, in particular the tragic and untimely death of his youngest daughter. Even for those who start out with a strong faith, sadness, loss, grief and pain can bring them to a place of absolute atheism.

Where was God when …?

How could God allow …?

If God were truly God, then …

Our comfortable interpretation of Christianity can sometimes come to nothing and be 'outed' as a marriage of convenience when we face unfaithfulness, illness or abuse. Until we face it, suffering is an abstract concept. It is a thought or an idea in a book. But Romans 8:28 is not meant to be interpreted as 'All things work together for good and therefore nothing bad will happen to you'. Far from it. We know we *will* have trouble.

For some people it is not just the personal experience of suffering that causes them to doubt and question God's promised presence, but also the immense pain of others. We only need to open a newspaper or go online to see disturbing images of people in desperate plights. How does this affect us?

When travelling on an aeroplane we are told where the emergency exits are. We are told the safety procedures to follow should an issue arise with the engine. In the same way, it is helpful to prepare ourselves to face anything that comes at us in life, so that we do not collapse when crises occur. We need to know how to handle and prepare for suffering. The way to get ourselves fit for this is by getting ourselves deeply rooted in the truths of Scripture, by being accountable to strong and dependable Christians, and by being part of the Body of Christ locally. We are not meant to be superhuman! We are allowed and meant to cry if and when tragedy strikes. However, it is possible to be rocked humanly, but remain steady spiritually.

Even in the midst of sin, pain, grief, war and famine, God sets His plans, ideas and love into the hearts of humankind. Part of His character, part of His DNA, is revealed. We see great rises of faith and compassion under seemingly impossible circumstances.

The second-century saint Irenaeus and the twentieth-century philosopher John Hick talk a great deal about this, terming it 'soul-making'. Irenaeus saw the world as a 'soul-making place'. In this world, he argued, we could complete our development as children of God. He believed evil, suffering and hardship are necessary to aid this development. His view was that even natural disasters such as famine have a divine purpose – to develop qualities such as compassion, grace, beauty and charity, which would rise to the surface.

Rabbi Jonathan Sacks said after the Indonesian tsunami, 'The only adequate religious response is to say, "God, I do not know why this terrifying disaster has happened, but I do know what You want of us: to help the afflicted, comfort the bereaved, send healing to the injured, and aid those who have lost their livelihoods and homes.'[7]

Of course, we can find evidence that the scale of tragedy in natural disasters is partly attributable to humans. The richer, more developed world has the power to choose to help its poorer brothers and sisters build earthquake-resistant buildings and tsunami warning systems. But, by and large, as someone has said, instead it prefers to buy artwork and holiday homes.

The truth is, we don't know why God allows suffering. We can argue the philosophies until we are blue in the face, and get nowhere. There are some things we will never know this side of heaven. As John Stott wrote:

> The Bible supplies no thorough solution to the problem of evil, whether natural evil or moral ... Its purpose is more practical than philosophical. Consequently, although there are references to sin and suffering on virtually every page, its concern is not to explain their origin but to help us overcome them.[8]

God works in mysterious ways. If God told us everything that was going to happen it might alleviate our fears, but it would also deprive us of the development of our faith and trust in Him. This is what brings our heavenly Father real joy: when we trust Him implicitly, even when we are faced with nothing but questions. Faith, after all, is the courage to live with uncertainty.

One of the lowest points for the children of Israel was when they were taken captive. God speaks to them in Isaiah 49 at this very darkest moment of their history and says, 'I will not forget you! See, I have engraved you on the palms of my hands' (Isa. 49:15–16). Even in the midst of uncertainty, God can be trusted. He is big enough. He is able. He is trustworthy, certain and sure. He can stand all of our questions, all of our doubts.

Just think how much shorter the Bible would be if it didn't contain questions or doubt! When we read the wonderful Psalms, we see how very real the language is. Life is not described as a bed of roses – there are complaints, tears, doubts, fears, sins and sorrows to deal with. The book of Psalms and the Bible as a whole really invite us into that uncertainty that may not have a resolution.

In addition, God never attempts to suppress our emotions, but rather encourages us to be real with Him. In Jeremiah 20:7, Jeremiah says to God,

> ... you deceived me ... I was deceived ... I am ridiculed all day long; everyone mocks me.

That sounds like a pretty harsh tirade to me. But does God knock Jeremiah back and say, 'You shouldn't be talking to me like that?' No. We don't find Him saying that at all. God soaks up Jeremiah's grievances and listens to him. After Jeremiah pours his heart out to God, he reflects again. The rush of emotion is out of the way, and he begins to remember the unmistakably clear call that came to him in his youth. That memory moves him and ministers to him. Something begins to burn within him again. The word of God returns to him and he allows it to penetrate into his being. God had hidden His word in Jeremiah's heart. It returned when he needed it. This is what we too need to do with Scripture. This is part of the reason why at CWR we have spent the last forty years trying to help people read and understand the Scriptures.

THE MYSTERY OF GOD'S STORY

> If terrible events are to constitute evidence that God does not exist, then every wonderful event, every cured cancer, every child rescued from a fire, every issue of love and devotion surely has to provide us with evidence that God *does* exist. The truth is that this is nonsense. My own view is that scepticism, at least in Britain, is more often than not the product of lazy thinking and apathy, not the result of conscious questioning of belief. It's not a tsunami or an earthquake that has undermined faith, but our reluctance to take seriously the fundamental questions of God's existence and our place in His story.[9]

That is the real challenge. Jesus walked amongst us in the flesh. He continually identified with those who were suffering; He identified with the bruised and the broken, the poor, the weak, the hopeless and the helpless. And this is where you and I come in. If we can learn to stand with and ache with and weep with those who suffer, we are being like Him.

Brennan Manning says:

> The gospels indicate, however, that at every moment of His life, Jesus was aware that everything came from the love of God. He never took His life for granted, but each moment received it as a free gift from His Abba – Abba Father. The nameless gratitude that we feel after a narrow escape from injury or death or some life crisis … Jesus felt that every morning as He rose from His sleep. He lived without boredom. He lived without tranquilisers or anaesthesia to numb either the pain or the joy of human experience.[10]

From the very beginning, God's intention has been to be in relationship with us. Genesis chapters 2–3 tell the story of how we threw that relationship away and have been trying to recover ever since. But God has not given up on us. He has persisted with us. Job's longing for answers to his questions ceased when he discovered that God had simply drawn near to him. When we are in the midst of pain or anxiety, doubt or fear, we assume that we want definitive answers. But what we actually need more is simply God's presence, and the assurance that we are loved and that we are not alone. In some way, whatever suffering we experience or whatever mysterious pain we endure, we can be assured that He is Immanuel – the One who is with us.

> Suffering is not a question that demands an answer.
> It's not a problem that demands a solution.
> It's a mystery that demands a presence.
>
> **Anon**

life
WITH G⊕D

'What a different relationship begins to develop when you realize that God is head-over-heels in love with you. God is simply giddy about you. He just can't help loving you. And he loves you deeply, recklessly and extravagantly – just as you are.'

DAVID G. BENNER[1]

07

THE DECISION OF DEVOTION

One of the dangers we all face on our spiritual journey is that although we acknowledge we love God, we only communicate with Him in a very cerebral, dry and formulaic way. Our relationship with Him does not have to be this way. There is a very real beauty to discover in seeking and developing an intimacy with God as we walk beside Him. Our relationship and friendship with Him can be one not just of knowledge and depth, but also of excitement and intimacy.

There have been many twists and turns in the road for me as I have sought to develop such a relationship with the Father, and challenges have come as I have learnt to trust in times of light as well as darkness. It is sometimes far from comfortable being a Christian, but my experience has shown that it is never dull!

Relationships of any kind require a sense of discipline and intentionality. As Christians, we don't suddenly become the finished article the moment we turn to Christ. Many of us have a great number of issues for God to deal with. Our 'old nature', our hang-ups and insecurities, our flaws and failings as well as our gifts, skills and passions are all raw materials that take time for God to work with and transform, in order to make us what He intends us to be. We are on a journey of faith that takes effort and many small acts of the will in order to get closer to God.

I don't know if you've noticed, but I once heard somebody say that often when people first become a Christian they just can't get enough. Every service they attend is 'amazing'. Every person they meet is 'wonderful'. Every book they read is a revelation. If someone asks a new Christian if they want coffee they say, 'Yes please. Jesus flavoured!' Everything is about Jesus. Life is fresh and exciting. Just as it should be.

But what about after six months? What sustains Christian growth when those first flushes of excitement start to be replaced with the realisation that people are flawed and not everyone sees things quite like you do? Maybe you start to notice that they know the Bible much better than you and get disheartened, or maybe they use special words when they pray that make you feel like an outsider? Suddenly your prayer life goes from the language of praise ('Jesus, You are so brilliant!') to the language of despair ('Jesus, I am so rubbish!').

It is all too easy to lose our enthusiasm and start thinking of prayer, Bible-reading and fasting as chores, or as things only 'holy people' do and not something we can keep up with. We can label ourselves as 'not very good' at them, as if they are some kind of test. But the truth is, God does not see devotion to Him in this way at all. Consider this passage from Matthew:

> While Jesus was in Bethany in the home of a man known as Simon the Leper, a woman came to him with an alabaster jar of very expensive perfume, which she poured on his head as he was reclining at the table. When the disciples saw this, they were indignant. 'Why this waste?' they asked. 'This perfume could have been sold at a high price and the money given to the poor.' Aware of this, Jesus said to them, 'Why are you bothering this woman? She has done a beautiful thing to me.'
>
> Matt. 26:6–10

Many commentators have identified this as one of the most amazing deeds in all of the Gospels. Why? Because it reflects a devotion to

Christ that is at once utterly selfless and totally spontaneous. It must have been an amazing scene to witness, and it prompted one of the most incredible affirmations and commendations from Jesus. First He says to those who accused her of needless extravagance, 'Why are you bothering this woman? She has done a beautiful thing to me.' Then He goes on to say,

> 'I tell you the truth, wherever the gospel is preached throughout the world, what she has done will also be told, in memory of her.'
>
> **Mark 14:9**

Jesus deeply acknowledges this lavish expression of love. By contrast, His disciples are churlish and indignant. They make a snide comment about the perfume being wasted and moot the idea that it could have been sold and the money given to the poor instead. (How often do we hear people making similar comments, dressing them up in plausibly religious language like this, when actually they are simply uncomfortable, finding what is happening inappropriate or challenging and provoking?)

I can't think of any greater honour than being commended by Jesus in this way. Can you imagine Him looking at *you* and saying: 'You have done a beautiful thing for me!'? That would be quite something, wouldn't it? What was it about Mary that Jesus was applauding and loving so much? I think it was her total devotion and worship. She did not care that her act could be misunderstood by others or seen as extravagantly wasteful. She wanted to give her all, her best, to her Lord. When we realise just how much Jesus loves to receive our love and worship, we will want to spend more time with Him in prayer, and learning how to live in an intimate relationship with Him.

THE COST OF DEVOTION

You can't be devoted to something or someone easily. Devotion implies a profound level of dedication, loyalty and a giving up of time. Mary's anointing of Jesus with oil did not just have an emotional cost, but also a physical one. There would have been a hefty price tag on that jar of perfume. Some commentators have suggested that it was likely her pension provision for old age. This amount of pure nard was worth 300 denarii, the equivalent of more than a year's wages. This one act of worship was tantamount to her pouring out her entire life and life savings onto Him.

The Gospel of John gives us another clue as to how Mary's act of love may have been seen by those in attendance. He describes how she 'let down her hair', something a woman would only normally have done in front of her husband. She was not just risking her financial future, but also her reputation. How many of us would have done the same? Mary's dramatic act was more powerful than words. It demonstrated her love and her faith, her trust and her understanding of who Jesus was, why He had come and what He was about to do. Her devotion is both inspiring and humbling.

There may be a cost involved when we choose to serve Jesus. What does that cost look like for you? I am not necessarily thinking about finances, but time, effort and determination. As far as we know, Mary didn't cast out demons like the disciples. As far as we know, Mary wasn't the instigator of incredible miracles or mass revival. What she did was to love Jesus in a way that made a difference to *Him*.

Consider ways in which you today can express your heartfelt love and devotion to Him. Perhaps pause now and consider your personal response to this event in Jesus' life.

THE LANGUAGE OF DEVOTION

Song of Solomon 1:3 contains this beautiful truth:

> Pleasing is the fragrance of your perfumes; your name is
> like perfume poured out.

In a similar way to Mary's act of worship, we are called to show God how we feel about Him and His name. Her love showed that she understood what the name Jesus (*Jeshua*, Saviour) really meant. What does your worship say about *your* revelation of who God is? Sometimes it's about a declaration – saying something outspoken, faith-filled or countercultural, standing up and being counted. One of the triggers of the 1904 Welsh Revival was when a shy young girl stood up and declared, 'I love the Lord Jesus Christ with all my heart!' At that point, the force of God's presence and arrival was dramatic. It was like a cork coming out of a bottle. Somehow God heard that one declaration and it sparked a great outpouring of His power. What might God do if we spoke out our unreserved praise like this?

Sometimes it's not our money, but our inhibitions and fears that we need to give to God. Can I trust Him? How does He feel about me? Is He on my side? Does He always love me? Understanding the depth of God's commitment to us answers those questions. God is not someone who simply wants a vague association with us. He desires a close and passionate relationship. That can sound off-putting for some of us, especially those of us who are English and not exactly known for our passion. We are known for our stiff upper lip, our reserve and our sporting behaviour! And this is not just a male problem. I find people in the UK can often be very difficult to read. If an Italian (male or female) is in love, or angry for some reason, everyone in the whole street knows about it! Do you know how you can tell when an English person is really, really angry? They start to walk in small circles, and then eventually they say, 'I'm going to write a letter of complaint'!

But whatever our personality type and however we show our emotions (or lack of emotion), we need to recognise that we are loved by a wonderfully passionate God. How do you tell God how you feel? What kind of language do you use?

Most people look at Paul's letter to the Church in Rome as a really heavy, theological book – one that needs to be studied carefully, verse-by-verse, with a weighty dictionary on hand to refer to. It is true that there is much rich theology contained within it. But notice how many words there are expressing simple heartfelt devotion. Paul was clearly a deeply passionate man. Look at the doxology of Romans 11:33–36, for instance:

> Oh, the depth of the riches of the wisdom and knowledge
> of God!
> How unsearchable his judgments,
> and his paths beyond tracing out!
> 'Who has known the mind of the Lord?
> Or who has been his counsellor?'
> 'Who has ever given to God,
> that God should repay him?'
> For from him and through him and to him are all things.
> To him be the glory for ever! Amen.

Our *theology*, if truly understood, must surely lead to *doxology* – a hymn of praise to God for who He is and what He does. That is the whole point. God doesn't want a robotic obedience. He wants our passionate engagement.

The book of Hosea provides another interesting perspective. Amongst other things, it presents us with a picture of a God whose heart is yearning for His rebellious people. At this time, the Israelites had rejected Him, but He persists in His desire to be their God. Even when they are throwing His love back in His face, we read this amazing passage in Hosea 11: 8–9:

> 'How can I give you up, Ephraim? How can I hand you over, Israel? How can I treat you like Admah? How can I make you like Zeboiim? My heart is changed within me; all my compassion is aroused. I will not carry out my fierce anger, nor will I devastate Ephraim. For I am God, and not man – the Holy One among you.'

God is a passionate being, and His passion is like a deep well that never runs dry.

THE REASON FOR DEVOTION

Jesus speaks in very relational and passionate terms about us, His followers. John 14:23 says:

> 'If anyone loves me, he will obey my teaching. My Father will love him, and we will come to him and make our home with him.'

Love language like this is used throughout the Bible, particularly in the Gospels and epistles. Yet many of us are so taken up with the 'doing' of Christianity that we can forget it is all about Jesus. Perhaps we serve at church with the wrong motives at times. Perhaps we catch ourselves doing things just so we can feel good abut ourselves or boast to our friends. Or maybe we serve God just because it is something we have 'always done'. It is good to remind ourselves that more than anything else, God wants our love. He wants to make His home within us. Disciplines such as studying the Bible and praying are great things to do, but their value is diminished if they become routine and mechanical. What we need instead are times of genuine love, adoration and devotion spent in God's presence. The *how* is much less important than the *why*. The difficulty is when we lose sight of the real purpose of our quiet time with God – when we think of it as solely for our benefit when in reality it is about Him. Activity and intimacy are not mutually exclusive, of course, but any activity for Jesus should naturally stem from our intimacy with Him. It is by devotional development (and by that I mean a loving relationship that touches our emotions, not just our intellect) that we can be free of this kind of imbalance.

I often come across church leaders or theological students who are caught up with issues such as differing views on predestination and election, and other theological hot topics. I'm not saying those things aren't important and that we shouldn't discuss them, but they must not be allowed to push what is vital to one side. As C.S. Lewis said, 'Put first things first and you get second things thrown in. Put second things first you are likely to lose both.'[2] This thought is discussed in more detail in Selwyn Hughes's book *7 Laws of Spiritual Success*.[3]

MUTUAL DEVOTION

Jesus promises to reveal Himself in the context of committed relationship. He is not indiscriminately intimate. The scribes and the Pharisees were probably the most biblically educated people in the world, and yet they did not enter into any kind of close relationship with Jesus. They fought over theology, but they were not interested in sitting at Jesus' feet like Mary. Jesus was intimate with sinners, with Gentiles and with those who were willing to trust Him. He is just like this today. He loves it when we love Him! He is proud to call us His own. He delights in us. He enjoys us.

If ever Selwyn Hughes was asked what was the most important lesson he'd learned over his sixty years walking with God, he would nearly always answer that it was the realisation that Jesus isn't seeking merely a *personal* relationship, but an *intimate* relationship with us. He said he realised one day that he was loved by *The World's Greatest Lover*, and that realisation changed everything.

THE BENEFITS OF DEVOTION

We know that prayer and Bible reading are the foundations of our spiritual life. If you watch any kind of building project, the longest and slowest part of the build is when the foundations, which are unseen, are laid. Our Christian lives really rise or fall at the point of our devotions.

Loving someone deeply always has consequences. Even though our times of devotion are first and foremost for God, nonetheless there are benefits for us in loving God and applying ourselves in devotion to Him. 1) We grow in knowledge and understanding of His will, His ways, His wonders and His words. 2) We grow to be more like Him. 3) We receive His direction and His guidance. 4) We are equipped for the journey of faith.

What benefits does soaking ourselves in God's Word have for our lives?

- The Word of God makes us wise (Psa. 119:98–104)
- It enables our faith to grow and rise (Rom. 10:17)
- It is useful for teaching, rebuking, training and encouraging (2 Tim. 3:16)
- It gives us revelation (Psa. 119:130)
- It gives us both the armour and weapons we need for spiritual warfare (2 Cor. 10:4)

THE BARRIERS TO DEVOTION

One of the biggest reasons we can find it hard to spend time with God is because for so many reasons we struggle to ever even get started. We know the importance of establishing a daily time with God in order to develop in maturity, yet we succomb to every distraction and immediate pressure, and fail to give it pre-eminence in our lives. The alarm doesn't go off. The children wake in the night. The washing machine breaks down. The boss makes a last-minute demand. What is the first thing to go? It is often our time with Jesus.

Yet, Jesus Himself often withdrew to lonely, quiet places to pray (Luke 5:16). He knew how important His time with His Father was, for many reasons, including giving Him strength to resist the enemy's advances and temptations. And when He was alone in the desert Jesus answered each of the devil's taunts with direct Scripture. He knew that the Word of God was the most powerful weapon He could fight with. Similarly, we must know God's Word and hide it deep within our hearts for times when we will need to sing out its truth.

When Moses had a meeting with God, recounted in Exodus 34:29, his appearance changed and his face became brighter and radiant, such was the impact of intimate time with his Father. Next time you are tempted to give up or close the door on spending time apart with God, stop and think. Whose voice are you listening to? Whose word are you believing?

We all know that at times, prayer, reading the Bible and fasting take discipline and effort. But every relationship requires intentionality if it is going to mature. No marriage would survive for long if the couple only had a conversation once every few months and hoped that would be enough to sustain it. Yet many of us live like that with God. We lurch from one church event or meeting to another, forgetting in between who we are and who God is.

THE DEVOTION OF PRAYER

Prayer is vital to our health! So here are some practical things to help you actually pray:

1. *Try to keep a journal.* Sometimes, especially when you are tired and discouraged, writing or re-reading your previous prayers will encourage you to pray again. If someone encourages you or gives you a word of Scripture, note it down and pray into it. God can use things spoken to us long after the person has said it, if we only remember to pray through it. Keep a note of things you learn and challenges you face, too. It helps to be specific in prayer.

2. *Write a prayer list.* Don't make it too long. Perhaps several names or situations each day for a week, with a few more on days when you have more time. Being realistic about praying helps you continue. Otherwise you might pray for two hours one day and then not at all for the next six months!

3. *Try to vary how you pray.* Sometimes people find it really helpful to pray in different positions. Kneeling, lying face down, standing up, or even leaning against a wall. Don't pray lying down under a duvet when you are tired – only one thing will happen and it won't be prayer! You might also like to try praying out loud or praying to music. Some people find that very helpful. There are now lots of CDs specifically designed to help you focus and pray.

4. *Listen to the Bible being read.* Sometimes it is good to hear Scripture on a CD or a DVD. Get yourself some worship resources to sing along to. God is not interested in how you sound, but in how your heart is before Him, so don't worry if you don't feel you are musical. That is not what matters at all.

5. *Try to make prayer a habit.* If you start each day in a certain way, add prayer to the list of ingredients. Many would agree that mornings are a good time. Work out a good time for you. Walking the dog, driving to work, having a shower … all these things can

be dedicated times to pray if we are a little creative with them.

6. *Pray with others you live with.* If you have children, maybe you could give them a routine of prayer that you help them with. Pray with them before they leave the house each day. Pray about things that bother you as a family, or that you are thankful for. Helping your children learn to pray can have the impact of reminding you to pray, too!

7. *Get yourself into a prayer partnership.* Your wife or husband, your friend or colleague – whoever God sends you. Meet with them and encourage them to pray through the things in their lives that need God's touch, and ask them to do the same for you.

8. *Try to pray naturally and don't put on a special 'praying voice'.* Engage God in the everyday things of life as well as the major things. Tell Him the realities of your life, in a real way.

All of this can sound very daunting, and I know that prayer is sometimes difficult. It is encouraging to remember that God's Spirit is right alongside us, helping us when we feel we don't know how or what to pray. He knows our heart and makes prayer out of our wordless sighs and our aching groans. He knows us far better than we know ourselves.

One of the things we have on occasion done at CWR, if we are praying for something in particular, is pray as we are making drinks for one another. A great deal of prayer goes on as the kettle is boiling in our building! It is a great way to remember to give things to God. I also find that if people ask me to pray about something, I do it there and then, otherwise I can all too easily just forget.

Pete Greig, in his book *God on Mute*[4], writes that he sets his watch to go off at midday every day, when he prays the Lord's Prayer. He says it is nearly always inconvenient and intrusive to do so, but that is a discipline in his life that God has blessed.

You need to be creative about finding times and ways to pray. One of the things some people do, for example, when ironing is to pray for the person whose clothes they are busily de-creasing.

FASTING AS A DEVOTIONAL TOOL

Many people find that fasting in the right way and for the right reasons, will bring them closer to God, and help them discover refreshing and new revelation from Him. Often, fasting also allows us to experience deeper fellowship with God. It can change our perspective on what we struggle with, and even bring new direction to our prayers. Fasting, in its literal sense, means abstaining from something for a time, normally food, in order to place our focus on God concerning any number of issues. Some people may choose to fast from alcohol, meat, television, chocolate or some other pleasure they enjoy. Interestingly the New Testament language clearly assumes believers *will* fast (see Matthew 6:16–18 and Mark 2:18–20, for example).

Here are some practical ideas to help you:

1. If you are going to start fasting for the first time, try just missing one meal and build up from there.
2. Always have plenty of water with you, to prevent dehydration and headaches.
3. Some people can fast for long periods. You may need to take some medical advice if you are considering a fast of longer than twenty-four hours. It may not be wise to fast if you are ill, on medication, pregnant, or driving long distances – we do need to apply common sense.
4. When fasting, try to keep it to yourself, unless someone makes a specific comment or needs to be informed not to make food for you. Otherwise it may appear we are trying to impress others with

our 'deep spirituality' (something the Bible warns us against; see Matthew 6:16–18).

5. When concluding a fast of twelve or more hours, eat a small amount for your initial meal because your stomach might not be ready for much. Avoid fatty foods as they might make you feel sick.

6. When you get hungry, turn those hunger pangs into prayer, asking God to satisfy you with the knowledge of His presence.

Set the period of time you want to fast for before you begin. The Bible doesn't stipulate how long we should fast for, so this is up to you and God. Your first few times may be a real battle, but don't give up! Ask God to give you perseverance. If you fail and break your fast before you meant to, try again. Perhaps fasting with a friend would help you maintain your fasting for the time you have set.

THE DEVOTION OF BIBLE READING

Bible reading is foundational to our devotional lives and aids our spiritual maturity, so here are some practical ideas to help us read our Bibles:

1. *Use Bible-reading notes.* There are many different kinds of Bible-reading materials available. Some are themed, some are based on journeying through a book in the Bible. If you don't already use something like this, I thoroughly recommend you try some out.

2. *Vary the translation you use.* Sometimes we get too familiar with hearing the same words. A new translation can have the impact of lifting the words off the page and making them live again. Try using the internet to help you with this – www.biblegateway. com is a site that will allow you to look up passages in different versions and languages giving fresh insight and understanding.

3. *Use a concordance.* Concordances and commentaries can help you dig deeper into the truths of Scripture. They are not meant for bedtime reading, but for studying the language and context of the passage in front of you.

4. *Keep a journal.* Writing down what you are learning means that you can meditate on it more easily and also keep a note of what God has spoken into your life.

5. *Go to a small group as part of your church.* Small groups will often do Bible study together. It can be helpful to talk about the Bible with other Christians, not just to gain their perspective but to share some of the lessons they have learnt.

6. *Listen to Podcasts of good messages.* There are some very good preachers and teachers who make their messages available to all via Podcasts. Check out some good sites and start listening to some extra teaching that blesses you and upholds the truth of the Bible.

7. *Memorise Scripture so that it is in your head and your heart.* Writing scriptures down and putting them in places where you will see them regularly will help. Some people find that putting verses to music helps. There are some Bible memory verse CDs to help you get Scripture into your mind.

8. *Consider going on a course.* It can be invaluable to receive deeper knowledge and understanding of the Bible, benefiting from the wide range of excellent courses and teaching materials now extensively available.[5]

There has never been more help for people really serious about understanding and knowing the Bible. One of the things that CWR has tried to do for the last forty years is to help and encourage people develop a rich devotional life. In the early *Every Day with Jesus* notes there was a phrase that stated, '*Every Day with Jesus* is an aid to personal revival'. God wants us all to experience a personal revival. Out of that personal revival can spread a national revival. I cannot stress strongly enough how key it is for you and I to develop our devotional lives. I don't just mean that we spend ten more minutes a day with our head buried in a concordance. It is important to see the whole of our lives – our job, the way we raise our children, the way we spend our money – as part of our devotion to God.

There is today much time and energy spent on maintaining or achieving physical and mental wellbeing. Whole industries have grown up around this important topic – being physically fit, eating a balanced diet and maintaining a healthy lifestyle; all, I must say, for good reason. We do need to take this topic seriously. Rarely would a serious or a competitive athlete enter a competition without preparation and training. And if we are to learn to live everyday life with God well we, too, need to be intentional.

More than anything else, God longs for a close and intimate relationship with us and, as we've seen, there are things we can do to develop this. Just as athletes train and discipline themselves to hone their skills and sensitivities to the task, we can engage in spiritual disciplines which will develop and build our spiritual lives – which in turn impact and influence every area of our lives.

Just as exercise strengthens the body, and studying strengths the mind, there are spiritual disciplines that increase our sensitivity to God; disciplines such as prayer, study, confession, worship, meditation, solitude, fasting, simplicity and stewardship. In this closing chapter we have only touched the surface of a few, and I encourage you to actively pursue and explore these further. They will all build and enhance your spiritual growth and life of devotion.

There is no doubt that this is challenging, *very challenging*! But it has to be said that where there is no challenge there is little change. So start where you are, just like any new routine or exercise and build up over time. But be intentional.

May God bless you as you seek to develop your own devotion to Him.

TRUST STEADILY, HOPE UNSWERVINGLY, LOVE EXTRAVAGANTLY

So we come to the final pages of our exploration of this journey of faith, hope, love and everything in between. Is this the end, or a brief pit stop for a change of tyres and a moment to catch our breath before continuing on our spiritual journey? I trust it's been an encouragement to you as we have travelled together.

Remember how often we need to encourage one another? We need to encourage one another daily in all these things that we often find difficult and that tend not to come naturally to us: issues of life that I consider must be navigated and faced if we are to grow in Christian maturity. We have looked at just a few; are there more? Absolutely! There are certainly not less. We've looked together at our world-view and how important it is to challenge our deeply imbedded ideas and values, as we've tried to answer that question – 'Who told you?' We've looked briefly at how we handle our relationships, what it means to be holy, living in the light of eternity, how we can learn to live with mystery and, finally, the foundational nature of spiritual disciplines such as prayer and study.

The prodigal son was prompted to begin *his* return journey when he remembered his father's goodness. It was then that he set off on his journey of hope. And as disciples of Jesus we too are on a journey of hope – our hope being the anticipation of full redemption.

The prodigal son, when he returns, finds the father watching and waiting for him. Whenever we wander off, or get distracted by the world's glittering lights and razzle dazzle, or, like John Bunyan's Pilgrim, we become trapped in despair, God is watching out for us and is waiting for us too – and we can, you can, trust Him to complete what He has started. Whatever it is that you may have remembered or maybe even discovered for the first time whilst reading this, you can trust Him to bring it to completion and maturity, because He is committed to working in your life.

We are on a journey of hope – and also of faith. Faith or trust is the remembrance of God's love.

And love: love is the invitation to know not just with our head but with our hearts; love is the invitation to know and experience the character of God.

And that's God's invitation to each and every one of us today; to join Him on this journey, to remember His goodness, to live in the hope of His saving grace and to know and experience the Father heart of God.

And so finally, I leave you with this last thought, from 1 Corinthians 13:8–13 (*The Message*):

> Love never dies. Inspired speech will be over some day; praying in tongues will end; understanding will reach its limit ... We don't yet see things clearly. We're squinting in a fog, peering through a mist. But it won't be long before the weather clears and the sun shines bright! We'll see it all then, see it all as clearly as God sees us, knowing Him directly just as He knows us! But for right now ... we have three things to do to lead us toward that consummation: Trust steadily in God, hope unswervingly, and love extravagantly.

NOTES

CHAPTER 1: LIFE'S JOURNEY

1. St Richard, twelfth-century Bishop of Chichester.
2. Rev Doctor John Montgomery, found on his blog: http://peopleoftheway.blogspot.com/2009/03/pilgrim's-way.html
3. Found on many websites.
4. Dallas Willard, *The Divine Conspiracy* (San Francisco: Harper, 1997).

CHAPTER 2: LIFE THROUGH A LENS

1. Mitch Albom, *Tuesdays with Morrie* (New York: Doubleday, 1997).
2. C.S. Lewis, *The Weight of Glory*, copyright © C.S. Lewis Pte. Ltd. 1980. Extract reprinted by permission.
3. C.S. Lewis, *Surprised by Joy* (Collins, 2011).
4. C.S. Lewis, *Mere Christianity* (Collins, 2011).
5. Philip Greenslade, *God's Questions* (CWR, 2003).
6. CWR's *Topz* daily Bible-reading notes are for 7- to 11-year olds.

CHAPTER 3: THE GOOD LIFE

1. H.G. Bosch, *Our Daily Bread* (Grand Rapids: RBC Ministries).
2. John Eldredge, *Knowing the Heart of God* (Thomas Nelson, 2009).
3. John Stott, *Confess Your Sins: The way of reconciliation* (Word, 1974).
4. A.W. Tozer, *The Attributes of God* (Wingspread, 2007).
5. Thomas Carlyle, from his lecture 'On the Choice of Books' delivered to students at Edinburgh University, 2 April 1866.
6. Rob Bell, from a talk 'Everything is Spiritual' – www.youtube.com
7. Dallas Willard, *Renovation of the Heart* (IVP, 2002).
8. M. Scott Peck, *The Road Less Traveled* (New York: Simon & Schuster, 1978).
9. Rowan Williams, from his sermon 'Holy Ground' published in *A Ray of Darkness: Sermons and Reflections* (Cowley Publications, 1995).
10. Gina Welch, *In the Land of the Believers* (New York: Metropolitan Books, 2010).
11. Anne Rice, *Called out of Darkness: A spiritual confession* (Chatto & Windus, 2008).
12. Ibid.
13. Philip Greenslade told this in his chapter in *Preach the Word* ed. Greg Haslam (Sovereign World, 2006).

CHAPTER 4: LIFE TOGETHER

1. C.S. Lewis, *The Four Loves*, copyright © C.S. Lewis Pte. Ltd. 1960. Extract reprinted by permission.
2. Larry Crabb as quoted in *Christ Empowered Living* by Selwyn Hughes (CWR, 2010).
3. Joann C. Jones, found on the web but we can find no original source.
4. Francis Gay, *The Friendship Book* (Dundee: DC Thomson & Co. Ltd., 2010).
5. Mary Kay Ash, *The Mary Kay Way* (John Wiley & Sons, 2008).
6. Gordon D. Fee, *Paul, the Spirit and the People of God* (Baker Academic, 1994).
7. Leo Buscaglia, *Loving Each Other – the challenge of human relationships* (Fawcett, 1st Ballantine Books traded edition, 1993).
8. David Kinnaman and Gabe Lyons, *UnChristian* (Grand Rapids: Baker, 2007).

CHAPTER 5: LIFE IN BETWEEN

1. Woody Allen, *Without Feathers* (London: Elm Tree Books, 1976).
2. A.J. Conyers, *The Eclipse of Heaven* (South Bend, IN: St Augustine's Press, 1999).
3. Malcolm Muggeridge, *Jesus Rediscovered* (Los Angeles, CA: Fount, 1976).
4. C.S. Lewis, *Mere Christianity* (London: HarperCollins, 2002).
5. Brent Curtis and John Eldredge, *The Sacred Romance: Drawing closer to the heart of God* (Thomas Nelson Publishers, May 1997).
6. Peter Kreeft, *Everything You Ever Wanted to Know About Heaven* (Ignatius Press, 1990).
7. Larry Norman, 'Reader's Digest' from the album *Only Visiting This Planet* (Solid Rock, 1972).
8. C.S. Lewis, *The Silver Chair* (London: HarperCollinsChildren's Books, 2001).
9. John Milton, *Paradise Lost* (London: Penguin Classics, 2003).
10. Stanley Hauerwas, William H. Willimon, *Resident Aliens* (Nashville, TN: Abingdon Press, 1993).
11. Ibid.
12. Rt Hon Sir Samuel Hoare, Viscount Templewood, *Ambassador on Special Mission* (London: Collins, 1946).

CHAPTER 6: LIFE'S BIG QUESTIONS

1. G.K. Chesterton, *Orthodoxy* (NuVision Publications, LLC, 2007).
2. Larry Crabb, *Soul Talk* (Thomas Nelson, 2005).
3. *The Guardian*, 'Weather men? They haven't got the foggiest' by Victoria Coren, 29 May 2010.
4. Hadron Collider, website: www.lhc.ac.uk
5. M. Scott Peck, *Newsweek*, March 1997.
6. Billy Graham, quoting from *Still Waters and Skyscrapers* by David Tomlinson (Baker Books, 2006).
7. Rabbi Jonathan Sacks, from *The Times*, 1 January 2005.
8. John Stott, *The Cross of Christ* (IVP, 2006).
9. *The Week*, January 2006.
10. Brennan Manning, *The Ragamuffin Bible* (Authentic Lifestyle, 2009).

CHAPTER 7: LIFE WITH GOD

1. David Benner, *The Gift of Being Yourself* (IVP, 2004).
2. C.S. Lewis, found in various of his writings including *Letters of C.S. Lewis*, copyright © C.S. Lewis Pte. Ltd. 1966. Extract reprinted by permission.
3. Selwyn Hughes, *7 Laws of Spiritual Success* (CWR, 2010).
4. Pete Greig, *God on Mute* (Eastbourne: Kingsway Publications, 2007).
5. For details of CWR courses and other resources to help you read and study the Bible visit: www.cwr.org.uk

National Distributors

UK: (and countries not listed below)
CWR, Waverley Abbey House, Waverley Lane, Farnham, Surrey GU9 8EP.
Tel: (01252) 784700 Outside UK (44) 1252 784700 Email: mail@cwr.org.uk

AUSTRALIA: KI Entertainment, Unit 21 317-321 Woodpark Road, Smithfield, New South Wales 2164. Tel: 1 800 850 777 Fax: 02 9604 3699 Email: sales@kientertainment.com.au

CANADA: David C Cook Distribution Canada, PO Box 98, 55 Woodslee Avenue, Paris, Ontario N3L 3E5. Tel: 1800 263 2664 Email: sandi.swanson@davidccook.ca

GHANA: Challenge Enterprises of Ghana, PO Box 5723, Accra. Tel: (021) 222437/223249 Fax: (021) 226227 Email: ceg@africaonline.com.gh

HONG KONG: Cross Communications Ltd, 1/F, 562A Nathan Road, Kowloon.
Tel: 2780 1188 Fax: 2770 6229 Email: cross@crosshk.com

INDIA: Crystal Communications, 10-3-18/4/1, East Marredpalli, Secunderabad – 500026, Andhra Pradesh. Tel/Fax: (040) 27737145 Email: crystal_edwj@rediffmail.com

KENYA: Keswick Books and Gifts Ltd, PO Box 10242-00400, Nairobi.
Tel: (254) 20 312639/3870125 Email: keswick@swiftkenya.com

MALAYSIA: Canaanland, No. 25 Jalan PJU 1A/41B, NZX Commercial Centre, Ara Jaya, 47301 Petaling Jaya, Selangor. Tel: (03) 7885 0540/1/2 Fax: (03) 7885 0545
Email: info@canaanland.com.my

Salvation Book Centre (M) Sdn Bhd, 23 Jalan SS 2/64, 47300 Petaling Jaya, Selangor.
Tel: (03) 78766411/78766797 Fax: (03) 78757066/78756360
Email: info@salvationbookcentre.com

NEW ZEALAND: KI Entertainment, Unit 21 317-321 Woodpark Road, Smithfield,
New South Wales 2164, Australia. Tel: 0 800 850 777
Fax: +612 9604 3699 Email: sales@kientertainment.com.au

NIGERIA: FBFM, Helen Baugh House, 96 St Finbarr's College Road, Akoka, Lagos.
Tel: (01) 7747429/4700218/825775/827264 Email: fbfm_1@yahoo.com

PHILIPPINES: OMF Literature Inc, 776 Boni Avenue, Mandaluyong City.
Tel: (02) 531 2183 Fax: (02) 531 1960 Email: gloadlaon@omflit.com

SINGAPORE: Alby Commercial Enterprises Pte Ltd, 95 Kallang Avenue #04-00, AIS Industrial Building, 339420. Tel: (65) 629 27238 Fax: (65) 629 27235
Email: marketing@alby.com.sg

SOUTH AFRICA: Struik Christian Books, 80 MacKenzie Street, PO Box 1144, Cape Town 8000. Tel: (021) 462 4360 Fax: (021) 461 3612
Email: info@struikchristianmedia.co.za

SRI LANKA: Christombu Publications (Pvt) Ltd, Bartleet House, 65 Braybrooke Place, Colombo 2. Tel: (9411) 2421073/2447665 Email: dhanad@bartleet.com

USA: David C Cook Distribution Canada, PO Box 98, 55 Woodslee Avenue, Paris, Ontario N3L 3E5, Canada. Tel: 1800 263 2664 Email: sandi.swanson@davidccook.ca

CWR is a Registered Charity – Number 294387
CWR is a Limited Company registered in England – Registration Number 1990308

Courses and seminars

Publishing and new media

Conference facilities

Transforming lives

CWR's vision is to enable people to experience personal transformation through applying God's Word to their lives and relationships.

Our Bible-based training and resources help people around the world to:
• Grow in their walk with God
• Understand and apply Scripture to their lives
• Resource themselves and their church
• Develop pastoral care and counselling skills
• Train for leadership
• Strengthen relationships, marriage and family life and much more.

Our insightful writers provide daily Bible-reading notes and other resources for all ages, and our experienced course designers and presenters have gained an international reputation for excellence and effectiveness.

CWR's Training and Conference Centre in Surrey, England, provides excellent facilities in an idyllic setting – ideal for both learning and spiritual refreshment.

 Applying God's Word *to everyday life and relationships*

CWR, Waverley Abbey House,
Waverley Lane, Farnham,
Surrey GU9 8EP, UK

Telephone: **+44 (0)1252 784700**
Email: **info@cwr.org.uk**
Website: **www.cwr.org.uk**

Registered Charity No 294387
Company Registration No 1990308

THIS GREAT TEACHING ALSO AVAILABLE ON DVD

Filmed on a variety of locations including a rally car, narrowboat, in an observatory and on the dance floor, this eye-opening DVD resource will help you to see more clearly that there is a divine pattern in place and a divine pacesetter walking with you.

Seven approximately 20-minute sessions cover:
• Life's Journey
• Life Through a Lens
• The Good Life
• Life Together
• Life In Between
• Life's Big Questions
• Life with God.

Great for small-group or individual use.

Faith, Hope, Love and Everything in Between DVD
Presented by Mick Brooks
EAN: 5027957001329

Also available at your church as a live seminar
For further information visit: www.cwr.org.uk/FHL

MANY PEOPLE THINK THE BIBLE IS BORING

But CWR daily devotionals are changing that!

Our range of daily Bible-reading notes has something for everyone – and to engage with even the most demanding members of the family!

Whether you want themed devotional writing, life-application notes, a deeper Bible study or meditations tailored to women or the growing minds of children and young people, we have just the one for you.

To order or for more information, including current prices, visit www.cwr.org.uk/store or a Christian bookshop.